Landmark
American Speeches

Volume II : The 19th Century

Maureen Harrison & Steve Gilbert
Editors

Excellent Books

Carlsbad, California College

EXCELLENT BOOKS
Post Office Box 131322
Carlsbad, CA 92013-1322

Publisher's Cataloging in Publication Data

Landmark American Speeches, Volume II: The 19th Century/
    Maureen Harrison, Steve Gilbert, editors.
    p. cm. - (Landmark Speeches Series)
Bibliography: p.

1. Speeches, addresses, etc., American.
I. Title. II. Harrison, Maureen. III. Gilbert, Steve.
IV. Series: Landmark Speeches Series.

PN6122. L235 2001   LC 98-72975
815.508 L235 -dc20
ISBN 1-880780-17-8

Introduction

Speak clearly if you speak at all;
Carve every word before you let it fall.
- Oliver Wendell Holmes, Sr.

Landmark American Speeches is a collection of outstanding American eloquence, clearly spoken public words, that allows readers to *hear* American history in the great words of extraordinary people.

The second volume of this collection, *Landmark American Speeches: The 19th Century*, presents thirty-four timeless speeches, each placed in its correct historic context by a complete biography of the speaker, a thorough history of the speech, and an extensive bibliography of the event.

In *Landmark American Speeches: The 19th Century*, the reader will find unforgettable speeches on the most important political, social, and moral questions of their times - Thomas Jefferson on democracy - *Though the will of the majority is in all cases to prevail, that will to be rightful must be reasonable.* Susan B. Anthony on women's suffrage - *We ask that all the civil and political rights that belong to citizens of the United States be guaranteed to us and our daughters forever.* Samuel Gompers on work - *Eight hours for sleep, eight hours for work, and eight hours for what we will.* Ralph Waldo Emerson on education - *Books are the best of things, well used; abused, among the worst.* Dorothea Dix on health - *God forbid that such another example of suffering should ever exist to be recorded.* Andrew Carnegie on wealth - *Not evil, but good, has come from the accumulation of wealth.* Henry David Thoreau on freedom - *Eastward I go only by force; but westward I go free.* Theodore Roosevelt on life - *I wish to preach, not the doctrine of ignoble ease, but the doctrine of the strenuous life.* Sojourner Truth on dignity - *I have borne thirteen chilern, and seen 'em mos' all sold off to slavery.*

Edited for readers, writers, and researchers, at all educational levels, *Landmark American Speeches* provides every librarian with a right-at-their-fingertips, one-stop reference.

Landmark American Speeches: The 19th Century presents to the readers the great words of Americans fighting other Americans for their freedom - Tecumseh, Chief of the Shawnee - *After such bitter events can you blame me for placing little confidence in the promises of Americans?* Feminist leader Elizabeth Cady Stanton - *We hold these truths to be self-evident - that all men and women are created equal.* Civil rights leader Frederick Douglass - *I will dare to call in question and to denounce everything that serves to perpetuate slavery - the great sin and shame of America!*

The war of words waged before, during, and after the American Civil War include those of - John Brown - *If it is deemed necessary that I should forfeit my life for the furtherance of the ends of justice . . . I say, let it be done.* Jefferson Davis - *If we may not hope to avoid war, we may at least expect that posterity will acquit us of having needlessly engaged in it.* Robert E. Lee - *I have determined to avoid the useless sacrifice of those whose past services have endeared them to their countrymen.* Abraham Lincoln - *With malice toward none, with charity for all, with firmness in the right, as God gives us to see the right, let us strive on to finish the work we are in - to bind up the nation's wounds, to care for him who shall have borne the battle, and for his widow, and his orphan.*

From Mark Twain's *Shameful Speech* to Nat Turner's *Confession,* and from William Jennings Bryan's electrifying *Cross Of Gold Speech* to Abraham Lincoln's immortal *Gettysburg Address,* this second volume of *Landmark American Speeches* is designed to be an easy-to-use, all-in-one, ready-reference library resource. Once a speech was selected for inclusion in *Landmark American Speeches,* the editors made every effort to either obtain the original text, or to reconcile differing texts, to provide the general adult and young adult reader the authentic words of the speakers. The only change we made to the texts is to carefully edit the essential sections presented into modern spelling and grammar.

Eloquence made Americans listen to these words. The ideas these *Landmark Speeches* contain have made them timeless.

- M.H. & S.G.

Table Of Contents

John C. Calhoun
The Nullification Crisis
36

The controversy is one between power and liberty; and I will tell the gentlemen who are opposed to me that, as strong as may be the love of power on their side, the love of liberty is still stronger on ours.

Andrew Carnegie
The Gospel Of Wealth
43

Not evil, but good, has come from the accumulation of wealth by those who have had the ability and energy to produce it.

Henry Clay
The Compromise Of 1850
50

I think that the Constitution of the thirteen States was made, not merely for the generation which then existed, but for posterity, undefined, unlimited, permanent, and perpetual.

Samuel Langhorne Clemens
Mark Twain's "Shameful" Speech
56

In my enthusiasm I may have exaggerated the details a little, but you will easily forgive me that fault, since I believe it is the first time I have ever deflected from perpendicular fact on an occasion like this.

Jefferson Davis
First Inaugural Address
62

If we may not hope to avoid war, we may at least expect that posterity will acquit us of having needlessly engaged in it.

Thomas Jefferson
First Inaugural Address
118

Though the will of the majority is in all cases to prevail, that will to be rightful must be reasonable, that the minority possess their equal rights, which equal law must protect.

Joseph, Chief of the Nez Perce
I Will Fight No More Forever
125

Hear me, my chiefs, I am tired. My heart is sad and sick. From where the sun now stands, I will fight no more forever.

Robert E. Lee
Farewell To The Confederate Army
127

I have determined to avoid the useless sacrifice of those whose past services have endeared them to their countrymen.

Abraham Lincoln
The Gettysburg Address
130

Fourscore and seven years ago our fathers brought forth on this continent a new nation, conceived in liberty, and dedicated to the proposition that all men are created equal.

Abraham Lincoln
Second Inaugural Address
130

With malice toward none, with charity for all, with firmness in the right, as God gives us to see the right, let us strive on to finish the work we are in - to bind up the nation's wounds, to care for him who shall have borne the battle, and for his widow, and his orphan.

Booker T. Washington
Cast Down Your Bucket Where You Are
211

"Cast down your bucket where you are" - cast it down in making friends, in every manly way, of the people of all races by whom we are surrounded.

Daniel Webster
The Plymouth Rock Oration
218

We have come to this Rock, to record here our homage for our Pilgrim Fathers - our sympathy in their sufferings, our gratitude for their labors, our admiration of their virtues, our veneration for their piety.

Frances Wright
American Patriotism
223

[The] patriot is a useful member of society, capable of enlarging all minds and bettering all hearts with which he comes in contact.

Chronological Table Of Speeches

To our friends

Mike and Georgette

John Quincy Adams
The Amistad Africans
February 24, 1841

All we want is make us free. - **The *Amistad* Africans**

In January 1839 Singbe-Piéh, a West African tribesman, was kidnapped. Called "Cinqué" by his Spanish-speaking captors, he was taken to the slave markets of Cuba, where he was auctioned off as a slave and loaded onto a Spanish ship named *Amistad* ("Friendship") for transport to a slave plantation. On the night of July 2, 1839, 49 Africans, led by Cinqué, revolted. They seized control of *Amistad*, killing some of the crew. On August 26 *Amistad*, adrift in the Atlantic, was seized by the U.S. Navy. The *Amistad* Africans, free for 55 days, were re-imprisoned. Spain demanded their immediate return, calling the *Amistad* Africans "pirates" and "murderers." President Van Buren refused to return them to Spain unless ordered to do so by a Federal Court. On January 13, 1840, a U.S. District Court decreed that the *Amistad* Africans be returned not to Spain but to Africa. In April 1840 the U.S. Court of Appeals affirmed the District Court's decision. An appeal was taken by the Spanish Government to the U.S. Supreme Court.

Former President John Quincy Adams was asked to represent the *Amistad* Africans. Known as "Old Man Eloquent," Adams was born on July 11, 1767 in Braintree, Massachusetts to John and Abigail (Smith) Adams. He had served as President Washington's Minister to the Netherlands, President Adams' Minister to Prussia, President Madison's Minister to England, President Monroe's Secretary of State, and as the sixth U.S. President.

On February 24, 1841, in Washington, D.C.'s Old Supreme Court Chamber, John Quincy Adams delivered this landmark speech, *The Amistad Africans.*

John Quincy Adams

May it please your Honors, in rising to address this Court as one of its attorneys and counselors, regularly admitted at a great distance of time, I feel that an apology might well be expected where I shall perhaps be more likely to exhibit at once the infirmities of age and the inexperience of youth, than to render those services to the individuals whose lives and liberties are at the disposal of this Court which I would most earnestly desire to render. But as I am unwilling to employ one moment of the time of the Court in anything that regards my own personal situation, I shall reserve what few observations I may think necessary to offer as an apology till the close of my argument on the merits of the question.

. . . . I derive consolation from the thought that this Court is a court of justice. And in saying so very trivial a thing, I should not on any other occasion, perhaps, be warranted in asking the Court to consider what justice is. Justice, as defined in the *Institutes of Justinian*, nearly 2000 years ago, and as it is felt and understood by all who understand human relations and human rights, is *the constant and perpetual will to secure all people's rights*.

And in a court of justice, where there are two parties present, justice demands that the rights of each party should be allowed to himself, as well as that each party has a right to be secured and protected by the Court. This observation is important, because I appear here on the behalf of thirty-six individuals, the life and liberty of every one of whom depend on the decision of this Court. The Court, therefore, I trust, in deciding this case, will form no lumping judgment on these thirty-six individuals, but will act on the consideration that the life and the liberty of every one of them must be determined by its decision for himself alone.

They are here, individually, under very different circumstances, and in very different characters. Some are in one predicament, some in another. In some of the proceedings by which they have been brought into the custody and under the protection of this Court, thirty-two or -three of them have been charged with the crime of murder. Three or four of them are female children, incapable, in the judgment of our laws, of the crime of murder or piracy, or, perhaps, of any other crime. Yet, from the day when the [slave-ship *Amistad*] was taken possession of by [the U.S. Navy], they have all been held as close prisoners, now for the period of eighteen long months, under custody and by authority of the Courts of the United States. I trust, therefore, that before the ultimate decision of this Court is established, its honorable members will pay due attention to the circumstances and condition of every individual concerned.

When I say I derive consolation from the consideration that I stand before a court of justice, I am obliged to take this ground, because, as I shall show, [the Executive] Department of the Government of the United States has taken, with reference to this case, the ground of utter injustice, and these individuals for whom I appear stand before this Court, awaiting their fate from its decision, under the array of the whole Executive power of this nation against them, in addition to that of a foreign nation. And here arises a consideration, the most painful of all others, in considering the duty I have to discharge, in which, in supporting the motion to dismiss the appeal, I shall be obliged not only to investigate and submit to the censure of this Court the form and manner of the proceedings of the Executive in this case, but the validity and the motive of the reasons assigned for its interference in this unusual manner in a suit between parties for their individual rights.

. . . . It is, therefore, peculiarly painful to me, under present circumstances, to be under the necessity of arraigning before this Court and before the civilized world the course of the existing Administration in this case. But I must do it. That Government is still in power, and thus subject to the control of the Court; the lives and liberties of all my clients are in its hands. And if I should pass over the course it has pursued, those who have not had an opportunity to examine the case and perhaps the Court itself might decide that nothing improper had been done, and that the parties I represent had not been wronged by the course pursued by the Executive. . . .

The charge I make against the present Executive administration is that in all their proceedings relating to these unfortunate men, instead of that *Justice*, which they were bound not less than this honorable Court itself to observe, they have substituted *Sympathy!* - sympathy with one of the parties in this conflict of justice, and *Antipathy* to the other. Sympathy with the white, antipathy to the black. . . .

All the proceedings of the government, Executive and Judicial, in this case had been founded on the assumption that the two Spanish slave-dealers were the only parties aggrieved - that all the right was on their side, and all the wrong on the side of their surviving self-emancipated victims. I ask your honors, was this *justice?* No. . . . It was sympathy [for the two Spanish slave-traders] deprived of their property and of their freedom, suffering from *lawless violence* in their persons, and in imminent and constant danger of being deprived of their lives also.

. . . . The sympathy of the Executive government, and as it were of the nation, in favor of the slave-traders, and against these poor, unfortunate, helpless, tongueless, defenseless Africans, was the cause and foundation and motive of all these proceedings, and has brought this case up for trial before your Honors.

. . . . The seizure of the [slave-ship *Amistad*], with the arrest and examination of the Africans, was intended for inquiry, and to lead to an investigation of the rights of all parties. This investigation has ultimated in the decision of the District Court, confirmed by the Circuit Court, which it is now the demand of the Executive should be reversed by this Court. The District Court has exercised its jurisdiction over the parties in interest, and has found that the right was with the other party, that the decisions of *Justice* were not in accordance with the impulses of sympathy, and that consequently the sympathy was wrong before. And consequently it now appears that everything which has flowed from this mistaken or misapplied sympathy was wrong from the beginning.

. . . . Is it possible that a President of the United States should be ignorant that the right of personal liberty is individual? That the right to it of every one, is *his own* . . . , and that no greater violation of his official oath to protect and defend the Constitution of the United States could be committed, than by an order to seize and deliver up at a foreign minister's demand thirty-six persons, in a mass, under the general denomination of *all*, the negroes, late of the *Amistad*? That he was ignorant, profoundly ignorant of this self-evident truth, inextinguishable till yonder gilt framed Declarations of Independence shall perish in the general conflagration of the great globe itself? I am constrained to believe - for to that ignorance, the only alternative . . . is willful and corrupt perjury to his official Presidential oath.

. . . . Was ever such a scene of Lilliputian trickery enacted by the rulers of a great, magnanimous, and Christian nation? Contrast it with that act of self-emancipation by which the savage, heathen barbarians Cinque and Grabeau liberated themselves and their fellow suffering countrymen from Spanish slave-traders, and which the [U.S.] Secretary of State, by communion of sympathy with [the Spanish slave-traders], denominates *lawless violence.* Cinque and Grabeau are uncouth and barbarous names. Call them Harmodius and Aristogiton, and go back for moral principle three thousand years to the fierce and glorious democracy of Athens. They too resorted to lawless violence, and slew the tyrant to redeem the freedom of their country. For this heroic action they paid the forfeit of their lives; but within three years the Athenians expelled their tyrants themselves, and in gratitude to their self-devoted deliverers decreed that thenceforth no slave should ever bear either of their names. Cinque and Grabeau are not slaves. Let them bear in future history the names of Harmodius and Aristogiton.

This review of all the proceedings of the Executive I have made with the utmost pain, because it was necessary to bring it fully before your Honors, to show that the course of that department had been dictated, throughout, not by *justice* but by *sympathy* - and a sympathy the most partial and unjust. And this sympathy prevailed to such a degree among all the persons concerned in this business as to have perverted their minds with regard to all the most sacred principles of law and right, on which the liberties of the people of the United States are founded; and a course was pursued, from the beginning to the end, which was not only an outrage upon the persons whose lives and liberties were at stake, but hostile to the power and independence of the judiciary itself.

I am now, may it please your Honors, obliged to call the attention of the Court to a very improper paper, in relation to this case, which was published in the *Official Journal* of the Executive Administration, on the very day of the meeting of this Court, and introduced with a commendatory notice by the editor, as the production of one of the brightest intellects of the South. I know not who is the author, but it appeared with that almost official sanction, on the day of meeting of this Court. It purports to be a review of the present case. The writer begins by referring to the decision of the District Court, and says the case is *one of the deepest importance to the Southern States*. I ask, may it please your Honors, is that an appeal to *Justice*? What have the Southern States to do with the case, or what has the case to do with the Southern States? The case, as far as it is known to the courts of this country, or cognizable by them, presents points with which the Southern States have nothing to do. It is a question of slavery and freedom between foreigners - of the lawfulness or unlawness of the African slave trade - and has not, when properly considered, the remotest connection with the interests of the Southern States.

What was the purpose or intent of that article, I am not prepared to say, but it was evidently calculated to excite prejudice, to arouse all the acerbities of feeling between different sections of this country, and to connect them with this case in such a manner as to induce this Court to decide it in favor of the alleged interests of the Southern States, and against the suppression of the African slave trade. It is not my intention to review the piece at this time. It has been done, and ably done, by more than one person. And after infinite difficulty, one of these answers has been inserted in the same *Official Journal* in which the piece appeared. I now wish simply to refer your Honors to the original principle of slavery, as laid down by this champion of the institution. It is given by this writer as a great principle of national law and stands as the foundation of his argument. I wish, if your Honors deem a paper of this kind, published under such circumstances, worthy of consideration in the decision of a case, that your Honors would advert to that principle, and say whether it is a principle recognized by this Court, as the ground on which it will decide cases.

The truth is that property in man has existed in all ages of the world, and results from the natural state of man, which is war. When God created the first family and gave them the fields of the earth as an inheritance, one of the number, in obedience to the impulses and passions that had been implanted in the human heart, rose and slew his brother. This universal nature of man is alone modified by civilization and law. War, conquest, and force, have produced slavery, and it is . . . the internal law of self-preservation that will ever perpetuate and defend it.

There is the principle, on which a particular decision is demanded from this Court, by the *Official Journal* of the Executive, on behalf of the Southern States. Is that a principle recognized by this Court? Is it the principle of that DECLARATION? [Here Adams pointed to a copy of the Declaration of Independence hanging on the wall.] It is alleged in the *Official Journal* that war gives the right to take the life of our enemy, and that this confers a right to make him a slave, on account of having spared his life. Is that the principle on which these United States stand before the world? That DECLARATION says that every man is *endowed by his Creator with certain inalienable rights*, and that *among these are life, liberty, and the pursuit of happiness*. If these rights are inalienable, they are incompatible with the rights of the victor to take the life of his enemy in war, or to spare his life and make him a slave. If this principle is sound, it reduces to brute force all the rights of man. It places all the sacred relations of life at the power of the strongest. No man has a right to life or liberty if he has an enemy able to take them from him. There is the principle. There is the whole argument of this paper. Now I do not deny that the only principle upon which a color of *right* can be attributed to the condition of slavery is by assuming that the natural state of man is *War.* The bright intellect of the South clearly saw that without this principle for a corner stone he had no foundation for his argument. He assumes it therefore without a blush, as Hobbes assumed it to prove that government and despotism are synonymous words. I will not here discuss the right or the rights of slavery, but I say that the doctrine of Hobbes, that *War* is the natural state of man, has for ages been exploded, as equally disclaimed and rejected by the philosopher and the Christian. That it is utterly incompatible with any theory of human rights, and especially with the rights which the Declaration of Independence proclaims as self-evident truths. The moment you come to the Declaration of Independence, that every man has a right to life and liberty, an inalienable right, this case is decided. I ask nothing more in behalf of these unfortunate men than this Declaration. . . .

I said when I began this plea that my final reliance for success in this case was on this Court as a court of *Justice,* and in the confidence this fact inspired that, in the administration of justice, in a case of no less importance than the liberty and the life of a large number of persons, this Court would not decide but on a due consideration of all the rights, both natural and social, of *every one* of these individuals. I have endeavored to show that they are entitled to their liberty from this Court. I have avoided, purposely avoided, and this Court will do justice to the motive for which I have avoided, a recurrence to those first principles of liberty which might well have been invoked in the argument of this cause. I have shown that [the two Spanish slave-traders], the only parties in interest here, for whose sole benefit this suit is carried on by the Government, were acting at the time in a way that is forbidden by the laws of Great Britain, of Spain, and of the United States, and that the mere signature of the Governor General of Cuba ought not to prevail over the ample evidence in the case that these negroes were free and had a right to assert their liberty. I have shown that the papers in question are absolutely null and insufficient as passports for persons, and still more invalid to convey or prove a title to property.

. . . . [M]y argument in behalf of the captives of the *Amistad* is closed.

Afterward

Two and a half years after their kidnapping, the surviving *Amistad* Africans boarded a passenger ship for their return voyage. Departing from New York in November 1841 they arrived in Freetown, Sierra Leone in January 1842 and returned to their homes. Singbe-Piéh returned to his village only to find it destroyed, its people missing, dead or kidnapped, victims of a tribal war. He never found his wife or children. He died in 1879 and was buried at the Medni Mission, Sherbo Island, Sierra Leone.

John Quincy Adams returned to his seat in Congress where he worked tirelessly for the abolition of slavery until his death, in the House of Representatives, on February 23, 1848. On his tombstone is inscribed this epitaph,

A son, worthy of his Father,
A Citizen, shedding glory on his Country,
A Scholar ambitious to advance mankind,
This Christian sought to walk humbly,
In the sight of God.

John Quincy Adams

Selected Reading

Adams, John Q., *Argument of John Quincy Adams Before the United States Supreme Court in the Case of Cinqué, and Other Africans*, 1841.

———, *Memoirs of John Quincy Adams*, 1876.

American Anti-Slave Society, *The Trial of the African Captives*, 1839.

Barber, John, *A History of the Amistad Captives*, 1840.

Bemis, Samuel, *John Quincy Adams and the Union*, 1956.

Kromer, Helen, *The Amistad Mutiny*, 1971.

———, *The Amistad Revolt*, 1973.

Morse, John, *John Quincy Adams*, 1882.

Quincy, Josiah, *Memoir of the Life of John Quincy Adams*, 1858.

Seward, H., *Life and Public Services of John Quincy Adams*, 1849.

Movies

Spielberg, Steven, *Amistad*, 1998.

Susan B. Anthony
A Declaration Of Women's Rights
July 4, 1876

If particular care and attention is not paid to the Ladies, we are determined to foment a rebellion.   **- Abigail Adams (1776)**

Susan Brownell Anthony, who fomented Abigail Adams *rebellion*, was born on February 15, 1820 in Adams, Massachusetts, the daughter of Daniel and Susan (Read) Anthony. At a lecture in 1851 Anthony, then a full-time teacher and part-time political activist, met Elizabeth Cady Stanton. At the 1848 Seneca Falls Women's Rights Convention, Stanton delivered a landmark speech, *The Women's Declaration Of Sentiments* (see page 179), which Anthony greatly admired. Anthony and Stanton joined forces in what would become a lifelong collaboration for women's rights.

In 1865 Anthony and Stanton, in the name of their American Equal Rights Association, petitioned the Congress to add women to the proposed Fifteenth Amendment to the Constitution which, as drafted, would grant only to men full citizenship, including the right to vote. Congress refused. Anthony and Stanton persevered in their work.

In 1876, to celebrate America's first centennial, the City of Philadelphia hosted a National Centennial Exhibition whose centerpiece would be a reading in Independence Hall of the Declaration of Independence by a descendant of one of the Founding Fathers. Anthony and her compatriots drafted *with critical consideration of every word and sentence* *"The Women's Declaration of Rights and Articles of Impeachment Against the Government of the United States."*

On July 4, 1876, Susan B. Anthony, surrounded by the other Founding Mothers, stood on the steps of Philadelphia's Independence Hall and read this landmark speech, *A Declaration of Women's Rights.*

12

Susan B. Anthony

While the nation is buoyant with patriotism, and all hearts are attuned to praise, it is with sorrow we come to strike the one discordant note, on this one-hundredth anniversary of our country's birth. When subjects of kings, emperors, and czars from the old world join in our national jubilee, shall the women of the republic refuse to lay their hands with benedictions on the nation's head? Surveying America's exposition, surpassing in magnificence those of London, Paris, and Vienna, shall we not rejoice at the success of the youngest rival among the nations of the earth? May not our hearts, in unison with all, swell with pride at our great achievements as a people - our free speech, free press, free schools, free church, and the rapid progress we have made in material wealth, trade, commerce, and the inventive arts? And we do rejoice in the success, thus far, of our experiment of self-government. Our faith is firm and unwavering in the broad principles of human rights proclaimed in 1776, not only as abstract truths, but as the cornerstones of a republic. Yet we cannot forget, even in this glad hour, that while all men of every race and clime and condition have been invested with the full rights of citizenship under our hospitable flag, all women still suffer the degradation of disfranchisement.

The history of our country the past hundred years has been a series of assumptions and usurpations of power over woman, in direct opposition to the principles of just government acknowledged by the United States as its foundation, which are:

First. The natural rights of each individual.

Second. The equality of these rights.

Third. That rights not delegated are retained by the individual.

13

Susan B. Anthony

Fourth. That no person can exercise the rights of others without delegated authority.

Fifth. That the non-use of rights does not destroy them.

And for the violation of these fundamental principles of our government, we arraign our rulers on this Fourth day of July, 1876, and these are our articles of impeachment:

Bills of attainder have been passed by the introduction of the word *male* into all the State Constitutions, denying to women the right of suffrage, and thereby making sex a crime - an exercise of power clearly forbidden in Article 1, Sections 9 and 10, of the United States Constitution.

The writ of habeas corpus, the only protection against *lettres de cachet* and all forms of unjust imprisonment, which the Constitution declares *shall not be suspended, except when in cases of rebellion or invasion the public safety demands it,* is held inoperative in every State of the Union in case of a married woman against her husband - the marital rights of the husband being in all cases primary, and the rights of the wife secondary.

The right of trial by a jury of one's peers was so jealously guarded that States refused to ratify the original Constitution until it was guaranteed by the Sixth Amendment. And yet the women of this nation have never been allowed a jury of their peers - being tried in all cases by men, native and foreign, educated and ignorant, virtuous and vicious. Young girls have been arraigned in our courts for the crime of infanticide - tried, convicted, hanged - victims, perchance, of judge, jurors, advocates - while no woman's voice could be heard in their defense. . . .

Taxation without representation, the immediate cause of the rebellion of the colonies against Great Britain, is one of the grievous wrongs the women of this country have suffered during the century. Deploring war, with all the demoralization that follows in its train, we have been taxed to support standing armies, with their waste of life and wealth. Believing in temperance, we have been taxed to support the vice, crime, and pauperism of the liquor traffic. While we suffer its wrongs and abuses infinitely more than man, we have no power to protect our sons against this giant evil. . . .

Unequal codes for men and women. Held by law a perpetual minor, deemed incapable of self-protection, even in the industries of the world, woman is denied equality of rights. The fact of sex, not the quantity or quality of work, in most cases decides the pay and position; and because of this injustice, thousands of fatherless girls are compelled to choose between a life of shame and starvation. . . .

Special legislation for woman has placed us in a most anomalous position. Women invested with the rights of citizens in one section - voters, jurors, office-holders - crossing an imaginary line, are subjects in the next. In some States, a married woman may hold property and transact business in her own name; in others, her earnings belong to her husband. In some States, a woman may testify against her husband, sue and be sued in the courts; in others, she has no redress in case of damage to person, property, or character. In case of divorce on account of adultery in the husband, the innocent wife is held to possess no right to children or property, unless by special decree of the court. But in no State of the Union has the wife the right to her own person, or to any part of the joint earnings of the co-partnership during the life of her husband. . . .

Representation of woman has had no place in the nation's thought. Since the incorporation of the thirteen original

States, twenty-four have been admitted to the Union, not one of which has recognized woman's right of self-government. On this birthday of our national liberties, July Fourth, 1876, Colorado, like all her elder sisters, comes into the Union with the invidious word *male* in her Constitution.

Universal manhood suffrage, by establishing an aristocracy of sex, imposes upon the women of this nation a more absolute and cruel despotism than monarchy; in that, woman finds a political master in her father, husband, brother, son. The aristocracies of the old world are based upon birth, wealth, refinement, education, nobility, brave deeds of chivalry - in this nation, on sex alone - exalting brute force above moral power, vice above virtue, ignorance above education, and the son above the mother who bore him.

The judiciary above the nation has proved itself but the echo of the party in power, by upholding and enforcing laws that are opposed to the spirit and letter of the Constitution. When the slave power was dominant, the Supreme Court decided that a black man was not a citizen, because he had not the right to vote; and when the Constitution was so amended as to make all persons citizens, the same high tribunal decided that a woman, though a citizen, had not the right to vote. Such vacillating interpretations of constitutional law unsettle our faith in judicial authority and undermine the liberties of the whole people.

These articles of impeachment against our rulers we now submit to the impartial judgment of the people. To all these wrongs and oppressions woman has not submitted in silence and resignation. From the beginning of the century, when Abigail Adams, the wife of one president and mother of another, said, *We will not hold ourselves bound to obey laws in which we have no voice or representation,* until now, woman's discontent has been steadily increasing, culminating nearly thirty years ago in a simultaneous movement among the women of the nation demanding the right of suffrage. In making our just demands, a higher motive than the pride of sex inspires us; we feel that national safety and stability depend on the complete recognition of the broad principles of our government. Woman's degraded, helpless position is the weak point in our institutions today - a disturbing force everywhere, severing family ties, filling our asylums with the deaf, the dumb, the blind, our prisons with criminals, our cities with drunkenness and prostitution, our homes with disease and death. It was the boast of the founders of the republic that the rights for which they contended were the rights of human nature. If these rights are ignored in the case of one-half the people, the nation is surely preparing for its downfall. Governments try themselves. The recognition of a governing and a governed class is incompatible with the first principles of freedom. Woman has not been a heedless spectator of the events of this century, nor a dull listener to the grand arguments for the equal rights of humanity. From the earliest history of our country, woman has shown equal devotion with man to the cause of freedom and has stood firmly by his side in its defense. Together, they have made this country what it is. Woman's wealth, thought, and labor have cemented the stones of every monument man has reared to liberty.

And now, at the close of a hundred years, as the hour-hand of the great clock that marks the centuries points to 1876, we declare our faith in the principles of self-government - our full equality with man in natural rights, that woman was made first for her own happiness, with the absolute right to herself - to all the opportunities and advantages life affords for her complete development; and we deny that dogma of the centuries, incorporated in the codes of all nations - that woman was made for man - her best interests in all cases to be sacrificed to his will. We ask of our rulers at this hour no special favors, no special privileges, no special legislation. We ask justice, we ask equality, we ask that all the civil and political rights that belong to citizens of the United States be guaranteed to us and our daughters forever.

Afterward

One of the Founding Mothers and most famous orators of the nineteenth century women's rights movement, Susan B. Anthony dedicated her life to obtaining equal rights for women. On November 5, 1872, in an act of civil disobedience, Anthony entered a Rochester, New York polling place and illegally voted. She was arrested. Free on bail, Anthony traveled the country delivering a lecture entitled *Is it a Crime for a United States Citizen to Vote?* Tried and convicted, she was fined $100. In response she told the Federal Judge, *I will never pay a dollar of your unjust penalty.* The fine remains, to this day, unpaid. On February 15, 1906, her 86th birthday, Anthony made her last speech, telling a gathering of women's rights activists, *There have been others just as true and devoted to the cause of women's rights - I wish I could name every one - but with such women consecrating their lives, failure is impossible!* Susan B. Anthony died on March 13, 1906. The Twentieth Amendment, guaranteeing women the right to vote, was enacted in 1919, fourteen years after her death. It is commonly called *The Susan B. Anthony Amendment.*

Selected Reading

Anthony, Katherine, *Susan B. Anthony: Personal History*, 1954.
Barry, Kathleen, *Susan B. Anthony: A Biography*, 1988.
Dorr, Rheta, *Susan B. Anthony*, 1928.
Harper, Ida, *The Life and Work of Susan B. Anthony*, 1908.
Lutz, Alma, *Susan B. Anthony*, 1959.

Black Elk, A Holy Man of the Oglala Sioux
The Butchering At Wounded Knee
December 29, 1890

Bury my heart at Wounded Knee. - **Stephen Vincent Benét**

The Great Sioux War was the losing struggle of the Sioux Nation against the U.S. Army for possession of the Dakota Territory. The second bloodiest day of that war was June 25, 1876, when, at the Battle of the Little Big Horn, 256 soldiers of the 7th Cavalry under the command of Colonel George Armstrong Custer were killed. The bloodiest day of the war was the Butchering at Wounded Knee.

Defeated Sioux tribes were exiled from their ancestral lands onto Indian reservations where, deprived of their way of life, they began to wither and die from disease, starvation, and hopelessness. In 1889 a holy man proclaimed himself the Ghost Dance Messiah. Through the ritual Ghost Dance, he prophesied that the red man would defeat the white man. The religious frenzy brought on by the Ghost Dance emboldened several Sioux tribes to leave the reservations to return to their ancestral lands.

On December 28, 1890, the 7th U.S. Cavalry surrounded an encampment of Sioux who had escaped the reservation and demanded their surrender. The Sioux, 350 in all (120 men and 230 women and children), were marched to the Wounded Knee Creek in present day South Dakota. There, on the morning of December 29, 1890, the 7th Cavalry opened fire and massacred over 300 Sioux. The Wounded Creek Massacre was the last battle of the Great Sioux War. Black Elk, a 27-year-old Oglala Sioux, heard the sound of gunfire on the morning of December 29, 1890 and reached Wounded Knee Creek just as the 7th Cavalry was leaving. This is his landmark account, *The Butchering At Wounded Knee.*

What we saw [at Wounded Knee Creek] was terrible. Dead and wounded women and children and little babies were scattered all along there where they had been trying to run away. The soldiers had followed along the gulch, as they ran, and murdered them in there. Sometimes they were in heaps because they had huddled together, and some were scattered all along. Sometimes bunches of them had been killed and torn to pieces where the [cannon] hit them. I saw a little baby trying to suck its mother, but she was bloody and dead.

. . . . Men and women and children were heaped and scattered all over the flat at the bottom of the little hill where the soldiers had their [cannon] and westward up the dry gulch all the way to the high ridge, the dead women and children and babies were scattered.

. . . . This is the way it was: . . . Soldiers were on the little hill and all around, and there were soldiers across the dry gulch to the south and over east along Wounded Knee Creek too. The people were nearly surrounded, and the [cannon] were pointing at them.

. . . . Then suddenly nobody knew what was happening, except that the soldiers were all shooting and the [cannons] began going off right in among the people.

Many were shot down right there. The women and children ran into the gulch and up west, dropping all the time, for the soldiers shot them as they ran. There were only about a hundred warriors and there were nearly five hundred soldiers. The warriors rushed to where they had piled their guns and knives. They fought soldiers with only their hands until they got their guns.

. . . . It was a good winter day when all this happened. The sun was shining. But after the soldiers marched away from their dirty work, a heavy snow began to fall. The wind came up in the night. There was a big blizzard, and it grew very cold. The snow drifted deep in the crooked gulch, and it was one long grave of butchered women and children and babies, who had never done any harm and were only trying to run away.

Afterwards

The Ghost Dance War ended on January 15, 1891 with the surrender of the Ghost Dance Prophet Kicking Bear. Wovoka, the Ghost Dance Messiah, died on October 4, 1932. Black Elk, Holy Man of Oglala Sioux, died on August 17, 1950.

Selected Reading

Black Elk, *Black Elk Speaks*, 1932.

Black Elk, Wallace H., and William S. Lyon, *Black Elk: The Sacred Ways of a Lakota*, 1991.

Brown, Dee, *Bury My Heart At Wounded Knee*, 1970.

Holler, Clyde, *Black Elk's Religion: The Sun Dance and Lakota Catholicism*, 1995.

Neihardt, John G., Editor, *Black Elk Speaks: Being the Life Story of a Holy Man of the Oglala Sioux*, 1988.

Rice, Julian, *Black Elk's Story: Distinguishing Its Lakota Purpose*, 1991.

Steltenkamp, Michael F., *Black Elk: Holy Man of the Oglala*, 1993.

Acknowledgement

This speech is reprinted from *Black Elk Speaks* by John G. Neihardt by permission of the University of Nebraska Press. Copyright 1932, 1959, 1972, by John G. Neihardt. Copyright 1961 by the John G. Neihardt Trust.

John Brown
Sentenced To Death
November 2, 1859

I, John Brown, am now quite certain that the crimes of this guilty land will never be purged away but with blood. I had as I now think vainly flattered myself that without very much bloodshed it might be done.
-John Brown, *Last Letter*, December 2, 1859

John Brown was born on May 9, 1800 in West Torrington, Connecticut, the son of Owen and Ruth (Mills) Brown. Early in life Brown turned all his energy to radical abolition, the political movement to bring an end to slavery by any means necessary. *A life committed to abolition,* wrote Brown in 1820, *would be nobly spent or sacrificed.*

On Sunday, October 16, 1859, John Brown, leading twenty-one followers, seized the U.S. arsenal at Harper's Ferry, Virginia. Brown called on the slaves in the area to join him and fight for their freedom. None did. The U.S. Marines, commanded by Colonel Robert E. Lee, rushed to the scene and stormed the arsenal. Brown was captured. Seventeen persons, including two of Brown's sons, were dead. John Brown's Raid had lasted thirty-six hours.

On October 25 Brown was indicted in a Virginia court on charges of treason, conspiracy, and murder. He told the judge, *If you seek my blood you can have it. I am ready for my fate. I do not ask for a trial. I beg for no mockery of a trial, no insult, nothing but that which conscience gives or cowardice would drive you to practice. I ask only that I may not be foolishly insulted as cowardly barbarians insult those who fall into their power.* The trial began the next day. On October 31, 1859, after 45 minutes of deliberation, the jury returned a verdict of guilty on all counts.

On November 2, 1859, John Brown, when asked if he had anything to say before the death sentence was imposed, stood before the court and delivered this landmark speech.

I have, may it please the Court, a few words to say. In the first place, I deny everything but what I have all along admitted of - a design on my part to free the slaves. I intended certainly to have made a clean thing of that matter, as I did last winter, when I went into Missouri and took slaves without the snapping of a gun on either side, moving them through the country and finally leaving them in Canada. I intended to do the same thing again on a larger scale. That was all I intended. I never did intend murder or treason or the destruction of property, or to excite or incite slaves to rebellion, or to make insurrection.

I have another objection, and that is that it is unjust that I should suffer such a penalty. Had I interfered in the manner which I admit, and which I admit has been fairly proved - for I admire the truthfulness and candor of the greater portion of the witnesses who have testified in the case - had I so interfered in behalf of the rich, the powerful, the intelligent, the so-called great, or in behalf of any of their friends, either father, mother, brother, sister, wife, or children, or any of that class, and suffered and sacrificed what I have in this interference, it would have been all right, and every man in this Court would have deemed it an act worthy of reward rather than punishment. This Court acknowledges too as I suppose the validity of the law of God. I see a book kissed, which I suppose to be the Bible (or at least the New Testament), which teaches me that all things whatsoever I would that men should do to me I should do so to them. It teaches me further to remember them that are in bonds as bound with them. I endeavored to act up to that instruction. I say that I am yet too young to understand that God is any respecter of persons. I believe that to have interfered as I have done, as I have always freely admitted I have done in behalf of his despised poor,

I did no wrong, but right. Now, if it is deemed necessary that I should forfeit my life for the furtherance of the ends of justice, and mingle my blood further with the blood of my children and with the blood of millions in this slave country whose rights are disregarded by wicked, cruel, and unjust enactments, I say, let it be done.

Let me say one word further. I feel entirely satisfied with the treatment I have received on my trial. Considering all the circumstances, it has been more generous than I expected. But I feel no consciousness of guilt. I have stated from the first what was my intention and what was not. I never had any design against the liberty of any person, nor any disposition to commit treason or incite slaves to rebel or make any general insurrection. I never encouraged any man to do so, but always discouraged any idea of that kind. Let me say also in regard to the statements made by some of those who were connected with me, I fear it has been stated by some of them that I have induced them to join me. But the contrary is true. I do not say this to injure them, but as regretting their weakness. No one but joined me of his own accord, and the greater part at their own expense. A number of them I never saw, and never had a word of conversation with till the day they came to me, and that was for the purpose I have stated. Now I have done.

Afterward

John Brown was executed on December 2, 1859. Abraham Lincoln, speaking on that day said, *We cannot object, even though he agreed with us in thinking slavery was wrong. That cannot excuse violence, bloodshed, and treason.* The war to end slavery, which John Brown wanted and Abraham Lincoln was to lead, began three years later.

John Brown

Selected Reading

Abels, Jules, *Man on Fire*, 1971.

Boyer, Richard, *The Legend of John Brown*, 1973.

DuBois, W.E.B., *John Brown*, 1909.

Karsner, David, *John Brown: Terrible Saint*, 1934.

Oates, Stephen, *To Purge This Land With Blood*, 1970.

Warren, Robert, *John Brown: The Making of a Martyr*, 1929.

William Jennings Bryan
The Cross Of Gold
July 13, 1896

The man who is employed for wages is as much a businessman as the merchant in New York. The farmer who goes forth in the morning and toils all day is as much a businessman as the man who goes upon the board of trade and bets upon the price of grain. The miner who goes down a thousand feet into the earth is as much a businessman as the few financial magnates who, in a back room, corner the money of the world. **- William Jennings Bryan (1894)**

On June 27, 1893, after twenty years on the Gold Standard (paper dollars backed by the price of gold), a stock market collapse, the *Panic of 1893*, threw the country into the worst depression in its history. 4,000,000 Americans - 20% of the work force - were unemployed. Thousands of small businesses and family farms failed as the gold-backed dollar fell in value.

On August 16, 1893, Nebraska Congressman William Jennings Bryan spoke in the House of Representatives, calling the Gold Standard-backed dollar a *dishonest dollar*. He called on the Government to abandon the *money powers'* Gold Standard and return to the *people's* Silver Standard. When the Government refused, Bryan began his campaign for the Democratic Party's 1896 Presidential nomination.

William Jennings Bryan, *The Great Commoner*, was born on March 19, 1860 in Salem, Illinois, the son of Silas and Mariah (Jennings) Bryan. Educated as a lawyer, and elected a Nebraska Congressman in 1890, he became the leader of the movement to replace gold dollars with silver.

On July 13, 1896, before a crowd of twenty thousand at the Democratic Convention in Chicago, William Jennings Byran made this landmark speech, *The Cross of Gold*.

Mr. Chairman and Gentlemen of the Convention, I would be presumptuous, indeed, to present myself against the distinguished gentlemen to whom you have listened if this were a mere measuring of abilities; but this is not a contest between persons. The humblest citizen in all the land, when clad in the armor of a righteous cause, is stronger than all the hosts of error. I come to speak to you in defense of a cause as holy as the cause of liberty - the cause of humanity.

When this debate is concluded, a motion will be made to lay upon the table the resolution offered in commendation of the Administration, and also the resolution offered in condemnation of the Administration. We object to bringing this question down to the level of persons. The individual is but an atom; he is born, he acts, he dies; but principles are eternal, and this has been a contest over a principle.

Never before in the history of this country has there been witnessed such a contest as that through which we have just passed. Never before in the history of American politics has a great issue been fought out, as this issue has been, by the voters of a great party. On the fourth of March, 1895, a few Democrats, most of them members of Congress, issued an address to the Democrats of the nation, asserting that the money question was the paramount issue of the hour, declaring that a majority of the Democratic party had the right to control the action of the party on this paramount issue, and concluding with the request that the believers in the free coinage of silver in the Democratic party should organize, take charge of, and control the policy of the Democratic party. Three months later, at Memphis, an organization was perfected, and the silver Democrats went forth openly and courageously proclaiming their belief, and declaring that, if successful, they would crystallize into a platform the declaration which they had made. Then began the conflict. With a zeal approaching the zeal which inspired the crusaders who followed Peter the Hermit, our silver Democrats went forth from victory unto victory, until they are now assembled, not to discuss, not to debate, but to enter up the judgment already rendered by the plain people of this country. In this contest brother has been arrayed against brother, father against son. The warmest ties of love, acquaintance, and association have been disregarded; old leaders have been cast aside when they have refused to give expression to the sentiments of those whom they would lead, and new leaders have sprung up to give direction to this cause of truth. Thus has the contest been waged, and we have assembled here under as binding and solemn instructions as were ever imposed upon representatives of the people.

. . . . The man who is employed for wages is as much a business man as his employer; the attorney in a country town is as much a businessman as the corporation counsel in a great metropolis; the merchant at the crossroads store is as much a businessman as the merchant of New York; the farmer who goes forth in the morning and toils all day - who begins in the spring and toils all summer - and who by the application of brain and muscle to the natural resources of the country creates wealth, is as much a businessman as the man who goes upon the board of trade and bets upon the price of grain; the miners who go down a thousand feet into the earth, or climb two thousand feet upon the cliffs and bring forth from their hiding places the precious metals to be poured into the channels of trade are as much businessmen as the few financial magnates who, in a back room, corner the money of the world. We come to speak for this broader class of businessmen.

Ah, my friends, we say not one word against those who live upon the Atlantic coast, but the hardy pioneers who have braved all the dangers of the wilderness, who have made the desert to blossom as the rose - the pioneers away out there, who rear their children near to Nature's heart, where they can mingle their voices with the voices of the birds - out there where they have erected schoolhouses for the education of their young, churches where they praise their Creator, and cemeteries where rest the ashes of their dead - these people, we say, are as deserving of the consideration of our party as any people in this country. It is for these that we speak. We do not come as aggressors. Our war is not a war of conquest; we are fighting in the defense of our homes, our families, and posterity. We have petitioned, and our petitions have been scorned; we have entreated, and our entreaties have been disregarded; we have begged, and they have mocked when our calamity came. We beg no longer; we entreat no more; we petition no more. We defy them.

The gentleman from Wisconsin has said that he fears a Robespierre. My friends, in this land of the free you need not fear that a tyrant will spring up from among the people. What we need is an Andrew Jackson to stand, as Jackson stood, against the encroachments of organized wealth.

They tell us that this platform was made to catch votes. We reply to them that changing conditions make new issues; that the principles upon which democracy rests are as everlasting as the hills, but that they must be applied to new conditions as they arise. Conditions have arisen, and we are here to meet these conditions. They tell us that the income tax ought not to be brought in here; that it is a new idea. They criticize us for our criticism of the Supreme Court of the United States. My friends, we have not criticized; we have simply called attention to what you already know. If you want criticisms, read the dissenting opinions of the court. There you will find criticism. They say that we passed an unconstitutional law; we deny it. The income tax law was not unconstitutional when it was passed; it was not unconstitutional when it went before the Supreme Court for the first time; it did not become unconstitutional until one of the judges changed his mind, and we cannot be expected to know when a judge will change his mind. The income tax is just. It simply intends to put the burdens of government justly upon the backs of the people. I am in favor of an income tax. When I find a man who is not willing to bear his share of the burdens of the government which protects him, I find a man who is unworthy to enjoy the blessings of a government like ours.

They say that we are opposing national bank currency. It is true. If you will read what Thomas Benton said, you will find he said that, in searching history, he would find but one parallel to Andrew Jackson - that was Cicero, who destroyed the conspiracy of Cataline and saved Rome. Benton said that Cicero only did for Rome what Jackson did for us when he destroyed the bank conspiracy and saved America. We say in our platform that we believe that the right to coin and issue money is a function of government. We believe it. We believe that it is a part of sovereignty, and can no more with safety be delegated to private individuals than we could afford to delegate to private individuals the power to make penal statutes or levy taxes. Mr. Jefferson, who was once regarded as good Democratic authority, seems to have differed in opinion from the gentleman who has addressed us on the part of the minority. Those who are opposed to this proposition tell us that the issue of paper money is a function of the bank, and that the Government ought to go out of the banking business. I stand with Jefferson rather than with them, and tell them, as he did, that the issue of money is a function of government, and that the banks ought to go out of the governing business.

They complain about the plank which declares against life tenure in office. They have tried to strain it to mean that which it does not mean. What we oppose by that plank is the life tenure which is being built up in Washington, and which excludes from participation in official benefits the humbler members of society.

Let me call your attention to two or three important things. The gentleman from New York says that he will propose an amendment to the platform providing that the proposed change in our monetary system shall not affect contracts already made. Let me remind you that there is no intention of affecting those contracts which according to present laws are made payable in gold; but if he means to say that we cannot change our monetary system without protecting those who have loaned money before the change was made, I desire to ask him where, in law or in morals, he can find justification for not protecting the debtors when the act of 1873 was passed, if he now insists that we must protect the creditors.

He says he will also propose an amendment which will provide for the suspension of free coinage if we fail to maintain the parity within a year. We reply that when we advocate a policy which we believe will be successful, we are not compelled to raise a doubt as to our own sincerity by suggesting what we shall do if we fail. . . . Our opponents have tried for twenty years to secure an international agreement, and those are waiting for it most patiently who do not want it at all.

And now, my friends, let me come to the paramount issue. If they ask us why it is that we say more on the money question than we say upon the tariff question, I reply that if protection has slain its thousands, the gold standard has slain its tens of thousands. If they ask us why we do not embody in our platform all the things that we believe in, we reply that when we have restored the money of the Constitution all other necessary reforms will be possible, but that until this is done there is no other reform that can be accomplished.

Why is it that within three months such a change has come over the country? Three months ago, when it was confidently asserted that those who believe in the gold standard would frame our platform and nominate our candidates, even the advocates of the gold standard did not think that we could elect a President. And they had good reason for their doubt, because there is scarcely a State here today asking for the gold standard which is not in the absolute control of the Republican party. But note the change. Mr. McKinley was nominated at St. Louis upon a platform which declared for the maintenance of the gold standard until it can be changed into bimetallism by international agreement. Mr. McKinley was the most popular man among the Republicans, and three months ago everybody in the Republican party prophesied his election. How is it today? Why, the man who was once pleased to think that he looked like Napoleon - that man shudders today when he remembers that he was nominated on the anniversary of the battle of Waterloo. Not only that, but as he listens he can hear with ever-increasing distinctness the sound of the waves as they beat upon the lonely shores of St. Helena.

Why this change? Ah, my friends, is not the reason for the change evident to anyone who will look at the matter? No private character, however pure, no personal popularity, however great, can protect from the avenging wrath of an indignant people a man who will declare that he is in favor of fastening the gold standard upon this country, or who is willing to surrender the right of self-government and place the legislative control of our affairs in the hands of foreign potentates and powers.

We go forth confident that we shall win. Why? Because upon the paramount issue of this campaign there is not a spot of ground upon which the enemy will dare to challenge battle. If they tell us that the gold standard is a good thing, we shall point to their platform and tell them that their platform pledges the party to get rid of the gold standard and substitute bimetallism. If the gold standard is a good thing, why try to get rid of it? . . . If the gold standard is a good thing we ought to declare in favor of its retention, and not in favor of abandoning it, and if the gold standard is a bad thing, why should we wait until other nations are willing to help us to let go? Here is the line of battle, and we care not upon which issue they force the fight; we are prepared to meet them on either issue or on both. If they tell us that the gold standard is the standard of civilization, we reply to them that this, the most enlightened of all the nations of the earth, has never declared for a gold standard and that both the great parties this year are declaring against it. If the gold standard is the standard of civilization, why, my friends, should we not have it? If they come to meet us on that issue we can present the history of our nation. More than that - we can tell them that they will search the pages of history in vain to find a single instance where the common people of any land have ever declared themselves in favor of the gold standard. They can find where the holders of fixed investments have declared for a gold standard, but not where the masses have.

Mr. Carlisle said in 1878 that this was a struggle between *the idle holders of idle capital* and *the struggling masses, who produce the wealth and pay the taxes of the country*, and, my friends, the question we are to decide is, upon which side will the Democratic party fight - upon the side of *the idle holders of idle capital*, or upon the side of *the struggling masses*? That is the question which the party must answer first. . . . The sympathies of the Democratic party, as shown by the platform, are on the side of the struggling masses, who have ever been the foundation of the Democratic party. There are two ideas of government. There are those who believe that if you will only legislate to make the well-to-do prosperous, their prosperity will leak through on those below. The Democratic idea, however, has been that if you legislate to make the masses prosperous, their prosperity will find its way up through every class which rests upon them.

You come to us and tell us that the great cities are in favor of the gold standard; we reply that the great cities rest upon our broad and fertile prairies. Burn down your cities and leave our farms, and your cities will spring up again as if by magic, but destroy our farms, and the grass will grow in the streets of every city in the country.

My friends, we declare that this nation is able to legislate for its own people on every question without waiting for the aid or consent of any other nation on earth, and upon that issue we expect to carry every State in the Union. . . . It is the issue of 1776 over again. Our ancestors, when but 3,000,000 in number, had the courage to declare their political independence on every other nation; shall we, their descendants, when we have grown to 70,000,000, declare that we are less independent than our forefathers? No, my friends, that will never be the verdict of our people. Therefore, we care not upon what lines the battle is fought. If they say bimetallism is good, but that we cannot have it until other nations help us, we reply that, instead of having a gold standard because England has, we will restore bimetallism, and then let England have bimetallism because the United States has it. If they dare to come out in the open field and defend the gold standard as a good thing, we will fight them to the uttermost. Having behind us the producing masses of this nation and the world, supported by the commercial interests, the laboring interests, and the toilers everywhere, we will answer their demand for a gold standard by saying to them - You shall not press down upon the brow of labor this crown of thorns; you shall not crucify mankind upon a cross of gold.

Afterward

After delivering *The Cross of Gold* speech, William Jennings Bryan captured the 1896 Democratic Presidential nomination but lost the general election. Bryan fought against the gold standard, abandoned in 1933; he also fought for a progressive federal income tax, adopted in 1913; prohibition, adopted in 1919; and woman's suffrage, adopted in 1920. William Jennings Bryan died in Dayton, Tennessee on July 26, 1925, after serving as prosecutor in the *Scopes Monkey Trial.*

Selected Reading

Anderson, David D., *William Jennings Bryan* , 1981.

Ashby, LeRoy, *William Jennings Bryan: Champion of Democracy*, 1987.

Bryan, William Jennings, *Speeches of William Jennings Bryan*, 1911.

Cherny, Robert W., *A Righteous Cause: The Life of William Jennings Bryan*, 1985.

Koenig, Louis, *Bryan: A Political Biography*, 1971.

Wilson, Charles M., *The Commoner: William Jennings Bryan*, 1970.

John C. Calhoun
The Nullification Crisis
February 15, 1833

The Union - next to our liberty most dear. May we all remember that it can only be preserved by respecting the rights of the States.
- John C. Calhoun, April 13, 1830

On July 14, 1832, President Andrew Jackson signed into law a protective tariff, called by those who opposed it the *Tariff of Abomination*. Tariffs, taxes on imports, helped the industrialized North and hurt the agricultural South. On November 24, 1832, South Carolina, in defiance of *King Andrew's Tariff*, adopted a Nullification Ordinance. Nullification, the theory that a State could declare Federal law null and viod, was the creation John C. Calhoun. On December 10, 1832, President Jackson issued a Proclamation warning South Carolina that their defiance would mean war.

John Caldwell Calhoun was born March 18, 1782 in Abbeville, South Carolina, the son of Patrick and Martha (Caldwell) Calhoun. Graduating from Yale, Calhoun served as a South Carolina Congressman, as President Monroe's Secretary of War, and as Vice President to both John Quincy Adams and Andrew Jackson. To find a peaceful solution to the nullification crisis, Calhoun resigned the Vice Presidency in 1832 to serve as South Carolina's U.S. Senator.

On January 16, 1833, President Jackson proposed a *Force Bill*, giving the Federal Government the right to use military power to enforce the tariff. Seeking a peaceful resolution of the nullification crisis, Calhoun announced support for Senator Henry Clay's *Compromise Tariff Bill*.

On February 15, 1833, John C. Calhoun spoke to the U.S. Senate in opposition to President Jackson's *Force Bill* in this landmark speech, *The Nullification Crisis*.

John C. Calhoun

Mr. President, I know not which is most objectionable, the provision[s of the Force Bill], or the temper in which its adoption has been urged. If the extraordinary powers with which the bill proposes to clothe the Executive, to the utter prostration of the Constitution and the rights of the States, be calculated to impress our minds with alarm at the rapid progress of despotism in our country, the zeal with which every circumstance calculated to misrepresent or exaggerate the conduct of [South] Carolina in the controversy is seized on with a view to excite hostility against her but too plainly indicates the deep decay of that brotherly feeling which once existed between these States. . . .

Has Congress the right to pass [the Force Bill]? The decision of this question involves the inquiry into the provisions of the bill. What are they? It puts at the disposal of the President the Army and Navy, and the entire militia of the country; it enables him, at his pleasure, to subject every man in the United States not exempt from militia duty to martial law - to call him from his ordinary occupation to the field and, under the penalty of fine and imprisonment inflicted by a court martial, to imbrue his hand in his brother's blood. There is no limitation on the power of the sword, and that over the purse is equally without restraint - for among the extraordinary features of the bill it contains no appropriation, which, under existing circumstances, is tantamount to an unlimited appropriation. The President may, under its authority, incur any expenditure, and pledge the national faith to meet it. He may create a new national debt at the very moment of the termination of the former - a debt of millions, to be paid out of the proceeds of the labor of that section of the country whose dearest Constitutional rights this bill prostrates! Thus exhibiting the extraordinary spectacle, that the very section of the country which is urging this measure, and carrying the sword of devastation against us, are at the same time incurring a new debt, to be paid by those whose rights are violated, while those who violate them are to receive the benefits in the shape of bounties and expenditures.

And for what purpose is the unlimited control of the purse and of the sword thus placed at the disposition of the Executive? To make war against one of the free and sovereign members of this Confederation, which the bill proposes to deal with, not as a State, but as a collection of banditti or outlaws - thus exhibiting the impious spectacle of this government, the creature of the States, making war against the power to which it owes its existence.

. . . . This bill proceeds on the ground that the entire sovereignty of this country belongs to the American people, as forming one great community, and regards the States as mere fractions or counties, and not as an integral part of the Union - having no more right to resist the encroachments of the government than a county has to resist the authority of a State, and treating such resistance as the lawless acts of so many individuals, without possessing sovereignty or political rights. It has been said that the bill declares war against South Carolina. No. It decrees a massacre of her citizens! War has something ennobling about it and, with all its honors, brings into action the highest qualities, intellectual and moral. It was, perhaps, in the order of Providence that it should be permitted for that very purpose. But this bill declares no war except, indeed, it be that which savages wage - a war not against the community, but the citizens of whom that community is composed. But I regard it as worse than savage warfare, as an attempt to take away life under the color of law without the trial by jury or any other safeguard which the Constitution has thrown around the life of the citizen! It authorizes the President, or even his deputies, when they may suppose the law to be violated, without the intervention of a court or jury, to kill without mercy or discrimination!

It has been said by the Senator from Tennessee to be a measure of peace! Yes, such peace as the wolf gives to the lamb, the kite to the dove! Such peace as Russia gives to Poland, or death to its victim! A peace by extinguishing the political existence of the State, by awing her into an abandonment of the exercise of every power which constitutes her a sovereign community. It is to South Carolina a question of self-preservation; and I proclaim it that, should this bill pass and an attempt be made to enforce it, it will be resisted at every hazard, even that of death itself. Death is not the greatest calamity; there are others still more terrible to the free and brave, and among them may be placed the loss of liberty and honor. There are thousands of her brave sons who, if need be, are prepared cheerfully to lay down their lives in defense of the State, and the great principles of Constitutional liberty for which she is contending. God forbid that this should become necessary! It never can be, unless this government is resolved to bring the question to extremity, when her gallant sons will stand prepared to perform the last duty - to die nobly.

I go on the ground that this Constitution was made by the States - that it is a federal union of the States, in which the several States still retain their sovereignty. If these views be correct, I have not characterized the bill too strongly, which presents the question whether they be or be not. . . .

I understood the Senator from Virginia to say that sovereignty was divided, and that a portion remained with the States severally, and that the residue was vested in the Union. By Union, I suppose the Senator meant the United

States. If such be his meaning, if he intended to affirm that the sovereignty was in the twenty-four States, in whatever light he may view them, our opinions will not disagree; but, according to my conception, the whole sovereignty is in the several States, while the exercise of sovereign powers is divided, a part being exercised under compact, through this General Government, and the residue through the separate State governments. But if the Senator from Virginia means to assert that the twenty-four States form but one community, with a single sovereign power as to the objects of the Union, it will be but the revival of the old question - of whether the Union is a union between States, as distinct communities, or a mere aggregate of the American people, as a mass of individuals; and in this light his opinions would lead directly to consolidation.

. . . . It is said that the bill ought to pass, because the law must be enforced. The law must be enforced. The imperial edict must be executed. It is under such sophistry, couched in general terms, without looking to the limitations which must ever exist in the practical exercise of power, that the most cruel and despotic acts ever have been covered. It was such sophistry as this that cast Daniel into the lion's den, and the three Innocents into the fiery furnace. Under the same sophistry the bloody edicts of Nero and Caligula were executed. The law must be enforced. Yes, the act imposing the *tea tax must be executed*. This was the very argument which impelled Lord North and his administration to that mad career which forever separated us from the British crown. Under a similar sophistry, *that religion must be protected*, how many massacres have been perpetrated? And how many martyrs have been tied to the stake? What! Acting on this vague abstraction, are you prepared to enforce a law without considering whether it be just or unjust, constitutional or unconstitutional? Will you collect money when it is acknowledged that it is not wanted? He who earns the money, who digs it from the earth with the sweat of his brow, has a just title to it against the universe. No one has a right to touch it without his consent except his government, and it only to the extent of its legitimate wants; to take more is robbery, and you propose by this bill to enforce robbery by murder. Yes - to this result you must come, by this miserable sophistry, this vague abstraction of enforcing the law, without a regard to the fact whether the law be just or unjust, constitutional or unconstitutional.

In the same spirit, we are told that the Union must be preserved, without regard to the means. And how is it proposed to preserve the Union? By force! Does any man in his senses believe that this beautiful structure, this harmonious aggregate of States, produced by the joint consent of all, can be preserved by force? Its very introduction will be certain destruction to this Federal Union. No, no. You cannot keep the States united in their Constitutional and federal bonds by force. Force may, indeed, hold the parts together, but such union would be the bond between master and slave - a union of exaction on one side, and of unqualified obedience on the other - that obedience which, we are told by the Senator from Pennsylvania, is the Union! Yes, exaction on the side of the master, for this very bill is intended to collect what can be no longer called taxes - the voluntary contribution of a free people - but tribute, tribute to be collected under the mouths of the cannon! Your customhouse is already transferred to a garrison, and that garrison with its batteries turned, not against the enemy of your country, but on subjects - I will not say citizens - on whom you propose to levy contributions. Has reason fled from our borders? Have we ceased to reflect? It is madness to suppose that the Union can be preserved by force. I tell you plainly that the bill, should it pass, cannot be enforced.

It will prove only a blot upon your statute book, a reproach to the year, and a disgrace to the American Senate. I repeat that it will not be executed; it will rouse the dormant spirit of the people, and open their eyes to the approach of despotism. The country has sunk into avarice and political corruption, from which nothing can arouse it but some measure, on the part of the government, of folly and madness, such as that now under consideration.

Disguise it as you may, the controversy is one between power and liberty; and I will tell the gentlemen who are opposed to me that, as strong as may be the love of power on their side, the love of liberty is still stronger on ours. . . .

Afterward

On March 2, 1833 President Andrew Jackson signed both the *Force Bill,* which gave him the right to enforce the Tariff, and the *Compromise Tariff Bill,* which, in effect, ended the Tariff. On March 11, 1833 South Carolina repealed the Nullification Ordinance and the crisis was ended.

John C. Calhoun died on March 31, 1850.

Selected Reading

Bancroft, Frederic, *Calhoun and the South Carolina Nullification Movement,* 1966.
Bartlett, Irving H., *John C. Calhoun: A Biography,* 1993.
Calhoun, John C., *The Papers of John C. Calhoun,* 1979.
Coit, Margaret L., Editor, *John C. Calhoun,* 1970.
Thomas, John L., Editor, *John C. Calhoun: A Profile,* 1968.
Wiltse, Charles, *John C. Calhoun,* 1944.

Andrew Carnegie
The Gospel Of Wealth
June 1, 1889

My chief happiness lies in the thought that even after I pass away the wealth that came to me to administer as a sacred trust for the good of my fellow men is to continue to benefit humanity for generations.

-Andrew Carnegie (1911)

Andrew Carnegie was born on November 25, 1835 in Dunfermline, Scotland, the son of William and Margaret (Morrison) Carnegie. Immigrating to America in 1848, Carnegie found office work at the Pennsylvania Railroad, earning $1,800 a year. By 1868 he was an executive of the company, earning $56,000 a year. Speculating in stock, Carnegie built an investment portfolio worth over $400,000. One of those investments, a Pittsburgh iron foundry, began in 1872 to manufacture a new metal - steel.

America's Industrial Revolution was built out of Carnegie Steel. By 1900 the privately-owned company produced 3,000,00 tons of steel and made a profit of $40,000,000. Wall Street financier J. Pierpont Morgan, owner of competitor Federal Steel, approached Carnegie with a proposal to purchase Carnegie Steel, merge it with Federal Steel and, taking the combined companies public, create the world's largest company, U.S. Steel. On February 26, 1901, Carnegie Steel was sold. Andrew Carnegie's share was $225,000,000. After the contracts were signed, J.P. Morgan said, *Mr. Carnegie I want to congratulate you on becoming the world's richest man.*

The *world's richest man*, to the shock of rich men like J.P. Morgan, proceeded to give away his wealth. On June 1, 1889, Andrew Carnegie addressed his thoughts on wealth, the responsibility of the wealthy, and the need for philanthropy in his landmark speech, *The Gospel Of Wealth*.

Objections to the foundations upon which society is based are not in order, because the condition of the race is better with these than with any others which have been tried. Of the effect of any new substitutes proposed we cannot be sure. The socialist or anarchist who seeks to overturn present conditions is to be regarded as attacking the foundation upon which civilization itself rests, for civilization took its start from the day when the capable, industrious workman said to his incompetent and lazy fellow, *If thou dost not sow, thou shalt not reap*, and thus ended primitive Communism by separating the drones from the bees. One who studies this subject will soon be brought face to face with the conclusion that upon the sacredness of property civilization itself depends - the right of the laborer to his hundred dollars in the savings bank, and equally the legal right of the millionaire to his millions. To those who propose to substitute Communism for this intense individualism, the answer therefore is - the race has tried that. All progress from that barbarous day to the present time has resulted from its displacement. Not evil, but good, has come to the race from the accumulation of wealth by those who have had the ability and energy to produce it. But even if we admit for a moment that it might be better for the race to discard its present foundation - individualism - that it is a nobler ideal that man should labor, not for himself alone, but in and for a brotherhood of his fellows, and share with them all in common - even admit all this, and a sufficient answer is - this is not evolution, but revolution. It necessitates the changing of human nature itself, a work of eons, even if it were good to change it, which we cannot know. It is not practicable in our day or in our age. Even if desirable theoretically, it belongs to another and long-succeeding sociological stratum. Our duty is with what is practicable now. . . .

It is criminal to waste our energies in endeavoring to uproot, when all we can profitably or possibly accomplish is to bend the universal tree of humanity a little in the direction most favorable to the production of good fruit under existing circumstances. We might as well urge the destruction of the highest existing type of man because he failed to reach our ideal as to favor the destruction of individualism, private property, the law of accumulation of wealth, and the law of competition, for these are the highest result of human experience, the soil in which society so far has produced the best fruit. Unequally or unjustly, perhaps, as these laws sometimes operate, and imperfect as they appear to the idealist, they are, nevertheless, like the highest type of man, the best and most valuable of all that humanity has yet accomplished.

We start, then, with a condition of affairs under which the best interests of the race are promoted, but which inevitably gives wealth to the few. Thus far, accepting conditions as they exist, the situation can be surveyed and pronounced good. The question then arises - and, if the foregoing be correct, it is the only question with which we have to deal - what is the proper mode of administering wealth after the laws upon which civilization is founded have thrown it into the hands of the few? And it is of this great question that I believe I offer the true solution. It will be understood that fortunes are here spoken of, not moderate sums saved by many years of effort, the returns from which are required for the comfortable maintenance and education of families. This is not wealth, but only competence, which it should be the aim of all to acquire.

There are but three modes in which surplus wealth can be disposed of. It can be left to the families of the decedents; or it can be bequeathed for public purposes; or finally, it can be administered during their lives by its possessors. Under the first and second modes most of the wealth of the world that has reached the few has hitherto been applied. Let us in turn consider each of these modes. The first is the most injudicious. In monarchical countries, the estates and the greatest portion of the wealth are left to the first son, that the vanity of the parent may be gratified by the thought that his name and title are to descend to succeeding generations unimpaired. The condition of this class in Europe today teaches the futility of such hopes or ambitions. The successors have become impoverished through their follies, or from the fall in the value of land. Even in Great Britain the strict law of entail has been found inadequate to maintain the status of an hereditary class. Its soil is rapidly passing into the hands of the stranger. Under republican institutions the division of property among the children is much fairer, but the question which forces itself upon thoughtful men in all lands is - why should men leave great fortunes to their children? If this is done from affection, is it not misguided affection? Observation teaches that, generally speaking, it is not well for the children that they should be so burdened. Neither is it well for the state. Beyond providing for the wife and daughters moderate sources of income, and very moderate allowances indeed, if any, for the sons, men may well hesitate, for it is no longer questionable that great sums bequeathed often work more for the injury than for the good of the recipients. Wise men will soon conclude that, for the best interests of the members of their families, and of the state, such bequests are an improper use of their means.

It is not suggested that men who have failed to educate their sons to earn a livelihood shall cast them adrift in poverty. If any man has seen fit to rear his sons with a view to their living idle lives, or, what is highly commendable, has instilled in them the sentiment that they are in a position to labor for public ends without reference to pecuniary considerations, then, of course, the duty of the parent is to see that such are provided for in moderation. There are instances of millionaires' sons unspoiled by wealth, who, being rich, still perform great services in the community. Such are the very salt of the earth, as valuable as, unfortunately, they are rare. It is not the exception, however, but the rule, that men must regard; and, looking at the usual result of enormous sums conferred upon legatees, the thoughtful man must shortly say, *I would as soon leave my son a curse as the almighty dollar*, and admit to himself that it is not the welfare of the children, but family pride, which inspires these enormous legacies.

As to the second mode, that of leaving wealth at death for public uses, it may be said that this is only a means for the disposal of wealth, provided a man is content to wait until he is dead before he becomes of much good in the world. Knowledge of the results of legacies bequeathed is not calculated to inspire the brightest hopes of much posthumous good being accomplished. The cases are not few in which the real object sought by the testator is not attained, nor are they few in which his real wishes are thwarted. In many cases the bequests are so used as to become only monuments of his folly. It is well to remember that it requires the exercise of not less ability than that which acquired the wealth to use it so as to be really beneficial to the community. Besides this, it may fairly be said that no man is to be extolled for doing what he cannot help doing, nor is he to be thanked by the community to which he only leaves wealth at death. Men who leave vast sums in this way may fairly be thought men who would not have left it at all, had they been able to take it with them. The memories of such cannot be held in grateful remembrance, for there is no grace in their gifts. It is not to be wondered at that such bequests seem so generally to lack the blessing.

The growing disposition to tax more and more heavily large estates left at death is a cheering indication of the growth of a salutary change in public opinion. The State of Pennsylvania now takes, subject to some exceptions, one-tenth of the property left by its citizens. The budget presented in the British Parliament the other day proposes to increase the death duties; and, most significant of all, the new tax is to be a graduated one. Of all forms of taxation, this seems the wisest. Men who continue hoarding great sums all their lives, the proper use of which for public ends would work good to the community, should be made to feel that the community, in the form of the state, cannot thus be deprived of its proper share. By taxing estates heavily at death the state marks its condemnation of the selfish millionaire's unworthy life.

It is desirable that nations should go much further in this direction. Indeed, it is difficult to set bounds to the share of a rich man's estate which should go at his death to the public through the agency of the state, and by all means such taxes should be graduated, beginning at nothing upon moderate sums to dependents, and increasing rapidly as the amounts swell. . . . This policy would work powerfully to induce the rich man to attend to the administration of wealth during his life, which is the end that society should always have in view, as being by far the most fruitful for the people. Nor need it be feared that this policy would sap the root of enterprise and render men less anxious to accumulate, for, to the class whose ambition it is to leave great fortunes and be talked about after their death, it will attract even more attention, and, indeed, be a somewhat nobler ambition to have enormous sums paid over to the state from their fortunes.

There remains, then, only one mode of using great fortunes, but in this we have the true antidote for the temporary unequal distribution of wealth, the reconciliation of the rich and the poor, a reign of harmony, another ideal, differing, indeed, from that of the Communist in requiring only the further evolution of existing conditions, not the total overthrow of our civilization. It is founded upon the present most intense individualism, and the race is prepared to put it in practice by degrees whenever it pleases. Under its sway we shall have an ideal state, in which the surplus wealth of the few will become, in the best sense, the property of the many, because administered for the common good; and this wealth, passing through the hands of the few, can be made a much more potent force for the elevation of our race than if it had been distributed in small sums to the people themselves. Even the poorest can be made to see this, and to agree that great sums gathered by some of their fellow citizens and spent for public purposes, from which the masses reap the principal benefit, are more valuable to them than if scattered among them through the course of many years in trifling amounts.

Afterward

Carnegie gave away most of his fortune, in excess of $350,000,000, to worthy causes. Andrew Carnegie died on August 11, 1919.

Selected Reading

Alderson, Bernard, *Andrew Carnegie: The Man and His Work*, 1909.

Bowman, John, *Andrew Carnegie: Steel Tycoon*, 1989.

Carnegie, Andrew, *Autobiography of Andrew Carnegie*, 1986.

Swetnam, George, *Andrew Carnegie*, 1980.

Wall, Joseph, *Andrew Carnegie*, 1970.

Henry Clay
The Compromise of 1850
February 6, 1850

Henry Clay's predominant sentiment, from first to last, was a deep devotion to the cause of human liberty.   **- Abraham Lincoln**

On February 2, 1848, at the end of the Mexican-American War, the United States acquired over 500,000 square miles of new territory. Southern States wanted Congress to extend the 1821 Missouri Compromise Line (slave states to the south, free states to the north) all the way to the Pacific Ocean. Northern States wanted *Popular Sovereignty*, allowing local voters, not Congress, to decide the question of slavery. The Union was threatened. Senator Henry Clay, who had twice before prevented disunion, attempted a third compromise to save the Union.

Henry Clay was born on April 12, 1777 in Hanover County, Virginia, the son of John and Elizabeth (Hudson) Clay. With only three years of formal education, 15-year-old Clay went to work, and study, in the offices of Judge George Wythe, the teacher of Thomas Jefferson and John Marshall. In 1797 Clay began to practice law in his adopted home state of Kentucky. Henry Clay's first public speech, an attack on President John Adams' Alien and Sedition Law, earned him local fame as a passionate orator. Elected to Congress in 1810, Clay earned national fame as the Great Compromiser by working out two settlements that kept the Union together - 1821's Missouri Compromise and 1833's Tariff Compromise. On January 29, 1850, Henry Clay introduced a new Compromise to defuse the current crisis. Neither the North nor South liked the Compromise but, to avert disunion, they agreed to debate its merits.

On February 6, 1850, Clay began the debate in the U.S. Senate with this landmark speech, *The Compromise of 1850.*

In my opinion there is no right on the part of one or more of the States to secede from the Union. War and the dissolution of the Union are identical and inseparable. There can be no dissolution of the Union, except by consent or by war. No one can expect, in the existing state of things, that that consent would be given, and war is the only alternative by which a dissolution could be accomplished. And, Mr. President, if consent were given, if possibly we were to separate by mutual agreement and by a given line, in less than sixty days after such an agreement had been executed, war would break out between the free and slaveholding portions of this Union - between the two independent portions into which it would be erected in virtue of the act of separation. Yes, sir, sixty days - in less than sixty days, I believe, our slaves from Kentucky would be fleeing over in numbers to the other side of the river, would be pursued by their owners, and the excitable and ardent spirits who would engage in the pursuit would be restrained by no sense of the rights which appertain to the independence of the other side of the river, supposing it, then, to be the line of separation. They would pursue their slaves, they would be repelled, and war would break out. In less than sixty days war would be blazing forth in every part of this now happy and peaceable land.

But how are you going to separate them? In my humble opinion, Mr. President, we should begin at least with three confederacies - the Confederacy of the North, the Confederacy of the Atlantic Southern States (the slaveholding States), and the Confederacy of the Valley of the Mississippi. My life upon it, sir, that vast population that has already concentrated, and will concentrate, upon the headwaters and tributaries of the Mississippi, will never consent that the mouth of that river shall be held subject to the power of any foreign State whatever. Such, I believe, would be the consequences of a dissolution of the Union. But other confederacies would spring up, from time to time, as dissatisfaction and discontent were disseminated over the country. There would be the Confederacy of the Lakes - perhaps the Confederacy of New England and of the Middle States.

But, sir, the veil which covers these sad and disastrous events that lie beyond a possible rupture of this Union is too thick to be penetrated or lifted by any mortal eye or hand.

Mr. President, I am directly opposed to any purpose of secession, of separation. I am for staying within the Union, and defying any portion of this Union to expel or drive me out of the Union. I am for staying within the Union and fighting for my rights - if necessary, with the sword - within the bounds and under the safeguard of the Union. I am for vindicating these rights, but not by being driven out of the Union rashly and unceremoniously by any portion of this Confederacy. Here I am within it, and here I mean to stand and die, as far as my individual purposes or wishes can go - within it to protect myself, and to defy all power upon earth to expel or drive me from the situation in which I am placed. Will there not be more safety in fighting within the Union than without it?

Suppose your rights to be violated; suppose wrongs to be done you, aggressions to be perpetrated upon you; can not you better fight and vindicate them if you have occasion to resort to that last necessity of the sword, within the Union, and with the sympathies of a large portion of the population of the Union of these States differently constituted from you, than you can fight and vindicate your rights, expelled from the Union, and driven from it without ceremony and without authority?

I said that I thought that there was no right on the part of one or more of the States to secede from this Union. I think that the Constitution of the thirteen States was made, not merely for the generation which then existed, but for posterity - undefined, unlimited, permanent, and perpetual - for their posterity, and for every subsequent State which might come into the Union, binding themselves by that indissoluble bond. It is to remain for that posterity now and forever. Like another of the great relations of private life, it was a marriage that no human authority can dissolve or divorce the parties from; and, if I may be allowed to refer to this same example in private life, let us say what man and wife say to each other, *We have mutual faults; nothing in the form of human beings can be perfect. Let us then be kind to each other, forbearing, conceding; let us live in happiness and peace.*

Mr. President, I have said what I solemnly believe - that the dissolution of the Union and war are identical and inseparable - that they are convertible terms.

Such a war, too, as that would be, following the dissolution of the Union! Sir, we may search the pages of history, and none so furious, so bloody, so implacable, so exterminating, from the wars of Greece down, including those of the Commonwealth of England, and the Revolution of France - none, none of them raged with such violence, or was ever conducted with such bloodshed and enormities, as will that war which shall follow that disastrous event - if that event ever happens - of dissolution.

And what would be its termination? Standing armies and navies, to an extent draining the revenues of each portion of the dissevered empire, would be created; exterminating wars would follow - not a war of two nor three years, but of interminable duration - an exterminating war would follow, until some Philip or Alexander, some Caesar or Napoleon, would rise to cut the Gordian knot, and solve the problem of the capacity of man for self-government, and crush the liberties of both the dissevered portions of this Union. Can you doubt it? Look at history - consult the pages of all history, ancient or modern; look at human nature - look at the character of the contest in which you would be engaged in the supposition of a war following the dissolution of the Union, such as I have suggested - and I ask you if it is possible for you to doubt that the final but perhaps distant termination of the whole will be some despot treading down the liberties of the people? - that the final result will be the extinction of this last and glorious light, which is leading all mankind, who are gazing upon it, to cherish hope and anxious expectation that the liberty which prevails here will sooner or later be advanced throughout the civilized world? Can you, Mr. President, lightly contemplate the consequences? Can you yield yourself to a torrent of passion, amid dangers which I have depicted in colors far short of what would be the reality, if the event should ever happen? I conjure gentlemen - whether from the South or the North, by all they hold dear in this world - by all their love of liberty - by all their veneration for their ancestors - by all their regard for posterity - by all their gratitude to Him who has bestowed upon them such unnumbered blessings - by all the duties which they owe to mankind, and all the duties they owe to themselves - by all these considerations I implore them to pause - solemnly to pause - at the edge of the precipice before the fearful and disastrous leap is taken in the yawning abyss below, which will inevitably lead to certain and irretrievable destruction.

And, finally, Mr. President, I implore, as the best blessing which Heaven can bestow upon me on earth, that if the direful and sad event of the dissolution of the Union shall happen, I may not survive to behold the sad and heart-rending spectacle.

Afterward

On July 6, 1850, at the close of the debate on the Compromise of 1850, Henry Clay spoke one last time, telling the Senate,

> *I believe from the bottom of my soul that this measure is the reunion of the Union. And now let us discard all resentments, all passions, all petty jealousies, all personal desires, all love of place, all hungering after the gilded crumbs which fall from the table of power. Let us forget popular fears, from whatever quarter they may spring. Let us go to the fountain of unadulterated patriotism, and, performing a solemn lustration, return divested of all selfish, sinister, and sordid impurities, and think alone of our God, our country, our conscience, and our glorious Union.*

On September 12, 1850, Congress enacted the Compromise of 1850.

Henry Clay died on June 29, 1852.

Selected Reading

Baxter, Maurice G., *Henry Clay and the American System*, 1995.
_____, *Henry Clay the Lawyer*, 2000.
Clay, Henry, *The Life and Speeches of Henry Clay*, 1987.
Remini, Robert V., *Henry Clay: Statesman for the Union*, 1991.
Schurz, Carl, *Henry Clay*, 1968.

Samuel Langhorne Clemens
Mark Twain's "Shameful" Speech
December 17, 1877

My pain and shame were so intense, and my sense of having been an imbecile so settled, established, and confirmed that I have lived in the conviction that my speech was coarse, vulgar, and destitute of humor.
- Mark Twain, *Autobiography*, January 11, 1906

On the night of December 17, 1877, New England's literary elite, including Ralph Waldo Emerson, William Wadsworth Longfellow, and Dr. Oliver Wendell Holmes, Sr., gathered for dinner at a Boston hotel to celebrate the seventieth birthday of John Greenleaf Whittier. The guest speaker was Mark Twain. He was introduced as *a humorist who never makes you blush to have enjoyed his joke.*

Samuel Langhorne Clemens, who wrote under the pen name Mark Twain, was born on November 30, 1835 in Florida, Missouri, the son of John and Jane (Langhorne) Clemens. At age fifteen he went to work on his brother's newspaper, the Hannibal, Missouri *Western Journal.* Under pen names such as *W. Epaminondas Adrastus Blab* and *Thomas Jefferson Snodgrass,* he began a lifelong career writing satirical articles. His travel lectures (*The American Vandal Abroad*), short stories (*The Celebrated Jumping Frog of Calaveras County*), and his books (including *The Innocents Abroad, The Gilded Age,* and *The Adventures of Tom Sawyer*), established Mark Twain's reputation as a brilliant speaker and satirist.

On the night of December 17, 1877, before a hundred invited guests, Mark Twain delivered this landmark speech in which Emerson, Longfellow, Holmes, and Twain all played a part. *I stood up,* Twain later wrote, *and at my genial and happy and self-satisfied ease began to deliver it.*

This is an occasion peculiarly meet for the digging up of pleasant reminiscences concerning literary folk; therefore, I will drop lightly into history myself. Standing here on the shore of the Atlantic and contemplating certain of its largest literary billows, I am reminded of a thing which happened to me thirteen years ago, when I had just succeeded in stirring up a little Nevadian literary puddle myself, whose spume-flakes were beginning to blow thinly Californiaward. I started an inspection tramp through the southern mines of California. I was callow and conceited, and I resolved to try the virtue of my *nom de guerre*.

I very soon had an opportunity. I knocked at a miner's lonely log cabin in the foothills of the Sierras just at nightfall. It was snowing at the time. A jaded, melancholy man of fifty, barefooted, opened the door to me. When he heard my nom de guerre he looked more dejected than before. He let me in, pretty reluctantly, I thought, and after the customary bacon and beans, black coffee, and hot whiskey, I took a pipe. This sorrowful man had not said three words up to this time. Now he spoke up and said, in the voice of one who is secretly suffering, "You're the fourth; I'm going to move." "The fourth what?" said I. "The fourth littery man that has been here in twenty-four hours; I'm going to move." "You don't tell me!" said I; "who were the others?" "Mr. Longfellow, Mr. Emerson, and Mr. Oliver Wendell Holmes, consound the lot!"

You can easily believe I was interested. I supplicated (three hot whiskeys did the rest), and finally the melancholy miner began. Said he, "They came here just at dark yesterday evening, and I let them in, of course. Said they were going to the Yosemite. They were a rough lot, but that's nothing; everybody looks rough that travels afoot. Mr. Emerson was a seedy little bit of a chap, red-headed. Mr. Holmes was as fat as a balloon; he weighed as much as three hundred, and had double chins all the way down to his stomach. Mr. Longfellow was built like a prizefighter. His head was cropped and bristly, like as if he had a wig made of hairbrushes. His nose lay straight down his face, like a finger with the end joint tilted up. They had been drinking - I could see that. And what queer talk they used! Mr. Holmes inspected this cabin, then he took me by the buttonhole, and says he, *Through the deep caves of thought/I hear a voice that sings/Build thee more stately mansions, O my soul!*

"Says I, 'I can't afford it, Mr. Holmes, and moreover I don't want to.' Blamed if I liked it pretty well, either, coming from a stranger, that way. However, I started to get out my bacon and beans, when Mr. Emerson came and looked on awhile, and then he takes me aside by the buttonhole and says, *Give me agates for my meat/Give me cantharids to eat/From air and ocean bring me foods/From all zones and altitudes.*

"Says I, 'Mr. Emerson, if you'll excuse me, this ain't no hotel.' You see it sort of riled me, I warn't used to the ways of littery swells. But I went on a-sweating over my work, and next comes Mr. Longfellow and buttonholes me, and interrupts me. Says he, *Honor be to Mudjekeewis!/You shall hear how Pau-Puk-Keewis.* But I broke in, and says I, 'Beg your pardon, Mr. Longfellow, if you'll be so kind as to hold your yawp for about five minutes and let me get this grub ready, you'll do me proud.' Well, sir, after they'd filled up, I set out the jug. Mr. Holmes looks at it, and then he fires up all of a sudden and yells, *Flash out a stream of blood-red wine!/For I would drink to other days.*

"By George, I was getting kind of worked up. I don't deny it - I was getting kind of worked up. I turns to Mr. Holmes, and says I, 'Looky here, my fat friend, I'm a-running this shanty, and if the court knows herself, you'll take whiskey straight or you'll go dry.' Them's the very words I said to him. Now I don't want to sass such famous littery people, but you see they kind of forced me. There ain't nothing unreasonable 'bout me; I don't mind a passel of guests a-treadin' on my tail three or four times, but when it comes to standing on it it's different, 'and if the court knows herself,' I says, 'you'll take whiskey straight or you'll go dry.' Well, between drinks they'd swell around the cabin and strike attitudes and spout; and pretty soon they got out a greasy old deck and went to playing euchre at ten cents a corner, on trust. I began to notice some pretty suspicious things. Mr. Emerson dealt, looked at his hand, shook his head, says, *I am the doubter and the doubt* and calmly bunched the hands and went to shuffling for a new layout. Says he, *They reckon ill who leave me out/They know not well the subtle ways I keep./I pass and deal again!*

"Hang'd if he didn't go ahead and do it, too! Oh, he was a cool one! Well, in about a minute things were running pretty tight, but all of a sudden I see by Mr. Emerson's eye he judged he had 'em. He had already corralled two tricks, and each of the others one. So now he kind of lifts a little in his chair and says, *I tire of globes and aces!/Too long the game is played!'* and down he fetched a right bower. Mr. Longfellow smiles as sweet as pie and says, *Thanks, thanks to thee, my worthy friend/For the lesson thou hast taught*, and blamed if he didn't down with another right bower! Emerson claps his hand on his bowie, Longfellow claps his on his revolver, and I went under a bunk. There was going to be trouble, but that monstrous Holmes rose up, wobbling his double chins, and says he, *Order, gentlemen; the first man that draws, I'll lay down on him and smother him! All quiet on the Potomac, you bet!*

"They were pretty how-come-you-so by now, and they begun to blow. Emerson says, *The nobbiest thing I ever wrote was "Barbara Frietchie."* Says Longfellow, *It don't begin with my*

59

"Biglow Papers." Says Holmes, *My "Thanatopsis" lays over 'em both.'* They mighty near ended in a fight. Then they wished they had some more company and Mr. Emerson pointed to me and says, *Is yonder squalid peasant all/ That this proud nursery could breed?.* He was a-whetting his bowie on his boot, so I let it pass. Well, sir, next they took it into their heads that they would like some music, so they made me stand up and sing "When Johnny Comes Marching Home" till I dropped, at thirteen minutes past four this morning. That's what I've been through, my friend. When I woke at seven, they were leaving, thank goodness, and Mr. Longfellow had my only boots on, and his'n under his arm. Says I, 'Hold on, there, Evangeline, what are you going to do with them?' He says, 'Going to make tracks with 'em; because, *Lives of great men all remind us/ We can make our lives sublime; And, departing, leave behind us/ Footprints on the sands of time.*

"As I said, Mr. Twain, you are the fourth in twenty-four hours, and I'm going to move; I ain't suited to a littery atmosphere."

I said to the miner, "Why, my dear sir, these were not the gracious singers to whom we and the world pay loving reverence and homage; these were impostors."

The miner investigated me with a calm eye for a while; then said he, "Ah! impostors, were they? Are you?"

I did not pursue the subject, and since then I have not traveled on my *nom de guerre* enough to hurt. Such was the reminiscence I was moved to contribute, Mr. Chairman. In my enthusiasm I may have exaggerated the details a little, but you will easily forgive me that fault, since I believe it is the first time I have ever deflected from perpendicular fact on an occasion like this.

Afterward

Mark Twain's satirical speech was met with total silence. *I wondered what the trouble was. I didn't know. I went on, hoping, but with gradually perishing hope, that somebody would laugh, or at least smile. But nobody did.* Twain apologized to Emerson, Longfellow, and Holmes the next day in a letter, saying, *I am a great and sublime fool. But then I am God's fool and all His works must be contemplated with respect.* Almost thirty years later Twain re-read *The Shameful Speech* and recanted his apology, writing, *The speech is as good as good can be. It is amazing, it is incredible, that they did not shout with laughter. Oh, the fault must have been with me, it is not in the speech at all.*

Mark Twain on died April 12, 1910.

Selected Reading

Blair, Walter, Editor, *Mark Twain's West: The Author's Memoirs About His Boyhood, Riverboats, and Western Adventures*, 1983.

Branch, Edgar M., *The Literary Apprenticeship of Mark Twain*, 1966.

Brashear, Minnie M., *Mark Twain, Son of Missouri*, 1964.

Brooks, Van Wyck, *The Ordeal of Mark Twain*, 1977.

Hoffman, Andrew, *Inventing Mark Twain*, 1997.

Kaplan, Justin, *Mr. Clemens and Mark Twain*, 1966.

Wiggins, Robert A., *Mark Twain, Jackleg Novelist*, 1964.

Jefferson Davis
First Inaugural Address
February 18, 1861

I, Jefferson Davis, do solemnly swear that I shall faithfully execute the office of President of the Confederate States of America, and will, to the best of my ability, preserve, protect, and defend the Constitution of the Confederate States of America. So help me God.

- Jefferson Davis' Presidential Oath of Office

On November 6, 1860, Abraham Lincoln, without receiving a single Southern electoral vote, was elected the President of the United States. Southern States, including Mississippi, seceded from the Union. On January 21, 1861, Mississippi's U.S. Senator Jefferson Davis resigned from the Senate to serve the Confederate States of America.

Jefferson Davis was born on June 3, 1808 near Hopkinsville, Kentucky, the son of Samuel and Jane (Cook) Davis. Educated at the U.S. Military Academy, Davis served in the Army before establishing *Brierfield,* his Mississippi cotton plantation. In the Mexican War, Davis commanded troops at the Battle of Buena Vista. On August 10, 1847, he was appointed Mississippi's U.S. Senator, a post he held until March 7, 1853, when President Franklin Pierce appointed him U.S. Secretary of War. Jefferson Davis returned to the U.S. Senate on March 4, 1857 and remained until his resignation.

On February 8, 1861, in Montgomery, Alabama, delegates from six seceded Southern States, meeting as the Provisional Confederate Congress, unanimously elected Jefferson Davis the first President of the Confederate States of America. Said one delegate, *The man and the hour have met.*

On February 18, 1861, Jefferson Davis, after taking the oath as President of the Confederate States of America, delivered this landmark speech.

Our present condition, achieved in a manner unprecedented in the history of nations, illustrates the American idea that governments rest upon the consent of the governed, and that it is the right of the people to alter and abolish governments whenever they become destructive to the ends for which they were established. The declared compact of the Union from which we have withdrawn was to establish justice, insure domestic tranquillity, provide for the common defense, promote the general welfare, and secure the blessings of liberty to ourselves and our posterity; and when in the judgment of the sovereign States now composing this Confederacy it has been perverted from the purposes for which it was ordained, and ceased to answer the ends for which it was established, a peaceful appeal to the ballot box declared that, so far as they were concerned, the government created by that compact should cease to exist. In this they merely asserted the right which the Declaration of Independence of 1776 defined to be inalienable. Of the time and occasion of this exercise they as sovereigns were the final judges, each for himself. The impartial, enlightened verdict of mankind will vindicate the rectitude of our conduct; and He who knows the hearts of men will judge of the sincerity with which we labored to preserve the government of our fathers in its spirit.

The right solemnly proclaimed at the birth of the States, and which has been affirmed and reaffirmed in the Bills of Rights of the States subsequently admitted into the Union of 1789, undeniably recognizes in the people the power to resume the authority delegated for the purposes of government. Thus the sovereign States here represented proceeded to form this Confederacy; and it is by the abuse of language that their act has been denominated revolution. They formed a new alliance, but within each State its government has remained. The rights of person and property have not been disturbed. The agent through whom they communicated with foreign nations is changed, but this does not necessarily interrupt their international relations. Sustained by the consciousness that the transition from the former Union to the present Confederacy has not proceeded from a disregard on our part of our just obligations or any failure to perform every constitutional duty, moved by no interest or passion to invade the rights of others, anxious to cultivate peace and commerce with all nations, if we may not hope to avoid war, we may at least expect that posterity will acquit us of having needlessly engaged in it. Doubly justified by the absence of wrong on our part, and by wanton aggression on the part of others, there can be no use to doubt the courage and patriotism of the people of the Confederate States will be found equal to any measure of defense which soon their security may require.

An agricultural people, whose chief interest is the export of a commodity required in every manufacturing country, our true policy is peace and the freest trade which our necessities will permit. It is alike our interest and that of all those to whom we would sell and from whom we would buy, that there should be the fewest practicable restrictions upon the interchange of commodities. There can be but little rivalry between ours and any manufacturing or navigating community, such as the northeastern States of the American Union. It must follow, therefore, that mutual interest would invite good will and kind offices. If, however, passion or lust of dominion should cloud the judgment or inflame the ambition of those States, we must prepare to meet the emergency, and maintain by the final arbitrament of the sword the position which we have assumed among the nations of the earth.

We have entered upon a career of independence, and it must be inflexibly pursued through many years of controversy with our late associates of the Northern States. We have vainly endeavored to secure tranquillity and obtain respect for the rights to which we were entitled. As a necessity, not a choice, we have resorted to the remedy of separation, and henceforth our energies must be directed to the conduct of our own affairs, and the perpetuity of the Confederacy which we have formed. If a just perception of mutual interest shall permit us peaceably to pursue our separate political career, my most earnest desire will have been fulfilled. But if this be denied us, and the integrity of our territory and jurisdiction be assailed, it will but remain for us with firm resolve to appeal to arms and invoke the blessing of Providence on a just cause. . . .

Actuated solely by a desire to preserve our own rights, and to promote our own welfare, the separation of the Confederate States has been marked by no aggression upon others, and followed by no domestic convulsion. Our industrial pursuits have received no check, the cultivation of our fields progresses as heretofore, and even should we be involved in war, there would be no considerable diminution in the production of the staples which have constituted our exports, in which the commercial world has an interest scarcely less than our own. This common interest of producer and consumer can only be intercepted by an exterior force which should obstruct its transmission to foreign markets, a course of conduct which would be detrimental to manufacturing and commercial interests abroad.

Should reason guide the action of the government from which we have separated, a policy so detrimental to the civilized world, the Northern States included, could not be dictated by even a stronger desire to inflict injury upon us;

but if it be otherwise, a terrible responsibility will rest upon it, and the suffering of millions will bear testimony to the folly and wickedness of our aggressors. In the meantime there will remain to us, besides the ordinary remedies before suggested, the well-known resources for retaliation upon the commerce of an enemy. . . . We have changed the constituent parts but not the system of our government. The Constitution formed by our fathers is that of these Confederate States. In their exposition of it, and in the judicial construction it has received, we have a light which reveals its true meaning. Thus instructed as to the just interpretation of that instrument, and ever remembering that all offices are but trusts held for the people, and that delegated powers are to be strictly construed, I will hope by due diligence in the performance of my duties, though I may disappoint your expectation, yet to retain, when retiring, something of the good will and confidence which will welcome my entrance into office.

It is joyous in the midst of perilous times to look around upon a people united in heart, when one purpose of high resolve animates and actuates the whole, where the sacrifices to be made are not weighed in the balance, against honor, right, liberty, and equality. Obstacles may retard, but they cannot long prevent, the progress of a movement sanctioned by its justice and sustained by a virtuous people. Reverently let us invoke the God of our fathers to guide and protect us in our efforts to perpetuate the principles which by his blessing they were able to vindicate, establish, and transmit to their posterity; and with a continuance of His favor, ever gratefully acknowledged, we may hopefully look forward to success, to peace, to prosperity.

Jefferson Davis

Afterward

Jefferson Davis served as the first and only President of the Confederate States of America. The Civil War ended in disaster for the South. Davis was imprisoned and charged with treason against the United States. The charge was dropped on February 15, 1869. On his seventy-third birthday, Davis' *The Rise and Fall of the Confederate Government* was published.

Jefferson Davis died on December 6, 1889.

Selected Reading

Alfriend, Frank H., *The Life of Jefferson Davis*, 1868.
Allen, Felicity, *Jefferson Davis, Unconquerable Heart*, 1999.
Davis, Burke, *The Long Surrender*, 1985.
Davis, Jefferson, *The Rise and Fall of the Confederate Government*, 1869.
Langhein, Eric, *Jefferson Davis, Patriot*, 1962.
Sanders, Phyllis M., *Jefferson Davis: Reactionary Rebel*, 1976.
Strode, Hudson, *Jefferson Davis: American Patriot*, 1955.

Dorothea Dix
The Suffering Insane
June 27, 1848

*I call your attention to the present state of insane persons confined in
cages, closets, cellars, stalls, and pens! Chained, naked, beaten, and
lashed into obedience.*   **- Dorothea Dix (1843)**

From pre-Revolutionary times, the *furiously mad, common luna-
tics, idiotic persons*, and *the pauper insane*, as American laws
termed the mentally ill, were committed to either medical
institutions - lunatic asylums (later called State hospitals) -
or confined in non-medical facilities for indigents and
criminals - poorhouses and jails.

Dorothea Lynde Dix, *The Voice For The Mad*, was born on
April 4, 1802 in Hampden, Maine, the daughter of Joseph
and Mary (Bigelow) Dix. While working as a schoolteacher,
Dix volunteered to teach Sunday School in the local jail. On
March 28, 1841, at the Cambridge House of Corrections,
Dorothea Dix witnessed the brutal conditions in which the
mentally ill were kept - *Scenes of horror and utter abomination
such as language is powerless to represent.*

Gathering around her physicians, clergymen, and social re-
formers, Dorothea Dix began a tireless lifelong effort to
reform the care and treatment of the mentally ill. Her initial
efforts on their behalf led to her first great victory, the
Massachusetts State Asylum Law, enacted on March 9, 1843.
Dix campaigned for reform in New England, the Midwest,
the Middle Atlantic, and the South, traveling over 10,000
miles and telling all who would listen, *I am an advocate for the
helpless, forgotten insane. Persons sunk to a condition from which the
most unconcerned individual would recoil with real horror.*

On June 27, 1848, Dorothea Dix's crusade for the suffering
insane reached Washington, D.C., where she delivered this
landmark speech to the United States Congress.

Dorothea Dix

I respectfully ask permission to lay before [the Congress] what seem to be just and urgent claims on behalf of a numerous and increasing class of sufferers in the United States. I refer to the great and inadequately relieved distresses of the insane throughout the country. . . .

I have myself seen [thousands of the] insane, in these United States, destitute of appropriate care and protection, and of this vast and most miserable company, sought out in jails, in poorhouses, and in private dwellings, there have been hundreds, nay, rather thousands, bound with galling chains, bowed beneath fetters and heavy iron balls, attached to dragchains, lacerated with ropes, scourged with rods, and terrified beneath storms of profane execrations and cruel blows - now subject to gibes, and scorn, and torturing tricks - now abandoned to the most loathsome necessities, or subject to the vilest and most outrageous violations. These are strong terms, but language fails to convey the astounding truths.

. . . . I offer but a single well-known example. In the yard of a poorhouse . . . I was conducted by the mistress of the establishment to a small building [housing an insane man]. . . . "Your [patient]. Where is he?" "You shall see, but stay outside till I get a lantern." Accustomed to exploring cells and dungeons in the basements and cellars of poorhouses and prisons, I concluded that the insane man spoken of was confined in some such dark, damp retreat. Weary and oppressed, I leaned against an iron door which closed the sole entrance to a singular stone structure, much resembling a tomb, yet its use in the courtyard of the poorhouse was not apparent. Soon, low smothered groans and moans reached me, as if from the buried alive. At this moment the mistress advanced, with keys and a lantern. "He's here," said she, unlocking the strong, solid iron door. A step down, and short turn through a narrow passage to the right, brought us, after a few steps, to a second iron door parallel to the first, and equally solid. In like manner, this was unlocked and opened, but so terribly noxious was the poisonous air that immediately pervaded the passage that a considerable time elapsed before I was able to return and remain long enough to investigate this horrible den. Language is too weak to convey an idea of the scene presented. The candle was removed from the scene, and the flickering rays partly illuminated a spectacle never to be forgotten. The place when closed had no source of light or of ventilation. It was about seven feet by seven, and six and a half high. All, even the roof, was of stone. An iron frame, interlaced with rope, was the sole furniture. The place was filthy, damp, and noisome; and the inmate, the crazy man, the helpless and dependent creature, cast by the will of Providence on the cares and sympathies of his fellowman, there he stood, near the door, motionless and silent; his tangled hair fell about his shoulders; his bare feet pressed the filthy, wet stone floor; he was emaciated to a shadow, etiolated, and more resembled a disinterred corpse than any living creature. Never have I looked upon an object so pitiable, so woe-struck, so imaging despair. I took his hands and endeavored to warm them by gentle friction. I spoke to him of release, of liberty, of care and kindness. Notwithstanding the assertions of the mistress that he would kill me, I persevered. A tear stole over the hollow cheek but no words answered to my importunities; no other movement indicated consciousness of perception or of sensibility. In moving a little forward I struck against something which returned a sharp metallic sound - it was a length of ox-chain, connected to an iron ring which encircled a leg of the insane man. At one extremity it was joined to what is termed a solid chain - namely, bars of iron

18 inches or 2 feet long, linked together, and at one end connected by a staple to the rock overhead. . . . "Sometimes he screams dreadfully," she added, "and that is the reason we had the double wall, and two doors in place of one. . . ." "How long has he been here?" "Oh, above three years, but then he was kept a long while in a cage first. But once he broke his chains and the bars, and escaped, so we had this built, where he can't get off." Get off! No, indeed - as well might the buried dead break through the sealed gates of the tomb, or upheave the mass of binding earth from the trodden soil of the deep grave. . . . God forbid that such another example of suffering should ever exist to be recorded.

. . . . I ask [the Congress] of the United States, with respectful but earnest importunity, assistance to the several States of the Union in providing appropriate care and support for the curable and incurable indigent insane.

. . . . Americans boast much of superior intelligence and sagacity, of power and influence, of their vast resources possessed and yet undeveloped, of their free institutions and civil liberty, of their liberally endowed schools of learning, and of their far-reaching commerce - they call themselves a mighty nation; they name themselves a great and wise people. If these claims to distinction above most nations of the earth are established upon undeniable premises, then will the rulers, the political economists, and the moral philosophers of other and remote countries look scrutinizingly into our civil and social condition for examples to illustrate the greatness of our name. They will seek not to measure the strength and extent of the fortifications which guard our coast; they will not number our vessels of war, or of commerce; they will not note the strength of our armies; they will not trace the course of the thousands eager for self-aggrandizement, nor of the tens of thousands led on by ambition and vainglory - they will search after illustrations in those God-like attributes which sanctify private life, and in that incorruptible integrity and justice which perpetuates national existence. They will note the moral grandeur and dignity which leads the statesman to lay broad and deep the foundations of national greatness, in working out the greatest good for the whole people - in effect, making paramount the interests of mind to material wealth, or mere physical prosperity. Primarily, then, in the highest order of means for confirming the prosperity of a people and the duration of government must be the education of the ignorant, and restoring the health and maintaining the sick mind in its natural integrity. . . .

Afterward

The *Dix Bill,* which would have set aside federal money for treatment of the suffering insane, was never brought to a vote in the 1848-49 Congressional Session. Resubmitted for each of the next four sessions, the *Dix Bill* failed to win approval. Finally in 1854 the U.S. Senate and House of Representatives passed the *Dix Bill,* only to have President Franklin Pierce veto it. He wrote, *If Congress has the power to make provisions for the indigent insane, it has the same power to provide for the indigent who are not insane, and thus transfer to the Federal Government the full charge of all the poor in all the States.*

Dorothea Dix worked the rest of her life as an advocate for the suffering insane. She died on July 17, 1887.

Dorothea Dix

Selected Reading

Brown, Thomas J., *Dorothea Dix: New England Reformer*, 1998.

Cooke, Frances E., *The Story of Dorothea Lynde Dix*, 1897.

Gollaher, David, *Voice for the Mad: The Life of Dorothea Dix*, 1995.

Lightner, David L., Editor, *Asylum, Prison, and Poorhouse: The Writings and Reform Work of Dorothea Dix in Illinois*, 1999.

Lowe, Corinne, *The Gentle Warrior*, 1948.

Marshall, Helen E., *Dorothea Dix, Forgotten Samaritan*, 1967.

Schlaifer, Charles, and Lucy Freeman, *Heart's Work: Civil War Heroine and Champion of the Mentally Ill, Dorothea Lynde Dix*, 1991.

Schleichert, Elizabeth, *The Life of Dorothea Dix*, 1992.

Tiffany, Francis, *Life of Dorothea Lynde Dix*, 1971.

Wilson, Dorothy C., *Stranger and Traveler: The Story of Dorothea Dix, American Reformer*, 1975.

Stephen Douglas
The First Lincoln-Douglas Debate
August 21, 1858

The Union was formed to establish justice and secure the blessings of liberty. When it fails to accomplish these ends, it will be worthless, and when it becomes worthless, it cannot long endure.

- Stephen Douglas, January 19, 1854

Stephen Arnold Douglas, called by friends and foes alike *The Little Giant*, was born on April 23, 1813 in Brandon, Vermont, the son of Stephen and Sarah (Fisk) Douglas. Admitted to the Illinois bar in 1834, Douglas was elected to the Illinois State Legislature in 1836. He served as Illinois Secretary of State, was appointed to the Illinois Supreme Court, and was elected to the U.S. House of Representatives. He was elected to the U.S. Senate in 1846.

By 1854 the Missouri Compromise of 1820 had became dangerously outdated. Senator Stephen Douglas proposed a replacement, the Kansas-Nebraska Act, which stated, *All questions pertaining to slavery in the Nebraska Territory, and in the new States of Kansas and Nebraska to be formed therefrom, are to be left to the decision of the people residing therein.* Under Douglas' Kansas-Nebraska Act, *Popular Sovereignty* allowed local voters, not Congress, to decide the question of slavery. The Kansas-Nebraska Act was enacted on May 26, 1854. The result, *Bloody Kansas*, was a disastrous small-scale civil war that so tarnished Douglas' reputation that ex-Congressman Abraham Lincoln was able to run against the politically weakened Douglas for his U.S. Senate seat in the election of 1858.

On August 21, 1858, in Ottawa, Illinois, Stephen Douglas began the first of the seven Lincoln-Douglas Debates with this landmark speech.

Prior to 1854 this country was divided into two great political parties, known as the Whig and Democratic parties. Both were national and patriotic, advocating principles that were universal in their application. An old-time Whig could proclaim his principles in Louisiana and Massachusetts alike. Whig principles had no boundary sectional line - they were not limited by the Ohio River, nor by the Potomac, nor by the line of the free and slave States, but applied and were proclaimed wherever the Constitution ruled or the American flag waved over the American soil.

So it was, and so it is with the great Democratic party, which, from the days of Jefferson until this period, has proven itself to be the historic party of this nation. While the Whig and Democratic parties differed in regard to a bank, the tariff distribution, the specie circular, and the subtreasury, they agreed on the great slavery question which now agitates the Union. I say that the Whig party and the Democratic party agreed on the slavery question, while they differed on those matters of expediency to which I have referred. The Whig party and the Democratic party jointly adopted the compromise measure of 1850 as the basis of a proper and just solution of the slavery question in all its forms. [Henry] Clay was the great leader, with [Daniel] Webster on his right and [Lewis] Cass on his left, and sustained by the patriots in the Whig and Democratic ranks who had devised and enacted the compromise measures in 1850.

In 1854 Mr. Abraham Lincoln and Mr. Lyman Trumbull entered into an arrangement, one with the other, and each with his respective friend, to dissolve the old Whig party on the one hand, and to dissolve the old Democratic party on the other, and to connect the members of both into an Abolition party, under the name and disguise of a Republican party. The terms of that arrangement between Lincoln and Trumbull have been published by Lincoln's special friend, James H. Matheny, Esq., and they were that Lincoln should have General Shield's place in the United States Senate, which was then about to become vacant, and that Trumbull should have my seat when my term expired. Lincoln went to work to abolitionize the old Whig party all over the State, pretending that he was then as good a Whig as ever; and Trumbull went to work in his part of the State preaching abolitionism in its milder and lighter form, and trying to abolitionize the Democratic party, and bring old Democrats handcuffed and bound hand and foot into the Abolition camp. In pursuance of the arrangement, the parties met at Springfield in October, 1854, and proclaimed their new platform. Lincoln was to bring into the Abolition camp the old-time Whigs, and transfer them over to Giddings, Chase, Fred Douglass, and Parson Lovejoy, who were ready to receive them and christen them in their new faith.

I desire to know whether Mr. Lincoln today stands as he did in 1854, in favor of the unconditional repeal of the Fugitive Slave Law. I desire him to answer whether he stands pledged today, as he did in 1854, against the admission of any more slave States into the Union, even if the people want them. I want to know whether he stands pledged against the admission of a new State into the Union with such a Constitution as the people of that State may see fit to make. I want to know whether he stands today pledged to the abolition of slavery in the District of Columbia. I desire him to answer whether he stands pledged to the prohibition of the slave trade between the different States. I desire to know whether he stands pledged to prohibit slavery in all the Territories of the United States, North as well as South of the Missouri Compromise line. I desire him to answer whether he is opposed to the acquisition of any more territory unless slavery is prohibited therein. I want his answer to these questions. Your affirmative cheers in favor of this Abolition platform are not satisfactory.

I ask Abraham Lincoln to answer these questions in order that when I trot him down to lower Egypt, I may put the same questions to him. My principles are the same everywhere. I can proclaim them alike in the North, the South, the East, and the West. My principles will apply wherever the Constitution prevails and the American flag waves. I desire to know whether Mr. Lincoln's principles will bear transplanting from Ottawa to Jonesboro. I put these questions to him today distinctly, and ask an answer. I have a right to an answer, for I quote from the platform of the Republican party, made by himself and others at the time that party was formed, and the bargain made by Lincoln to dissolve and kill the old Whig party, and transfer its members, bound hand and foot, to the Abolition party under the direction of Giddings and Fred Douglass.

In the remarks I have made on this platform, and the position of Mr. Lincoln upon it, I mean nothing personally disrespectful or unkind to that gentleman. I have known him for nearly twenty-five years. There were many points of sympathy between us when we first got acquainted. We were both comparatively boys, and both struggling with poverty in a strange land. I was a schoolteacher in the town of Winchester, and he a flourishing grocery keeper in the town of Salem. He was more successful in his occupation than I was in mine, and hence more fortunate in this world's goods. Lincoln is one of those peculiar men who perform with admirable skill everything which they undertake. I made as good a schoolteacher as I could and, when a cabinet maker, I made a good bedstead and tables, although my old boss said I succeeded better with bureaus and secretaries than with anything else; but I believe that Lincoln always was more successful in business than I, for his business enabled him to get into the Legislature.

I met him there, however, and had sympathy with him, because of the uphill struggle we both had in life. He was then just as good at telling an anecdote as now. He could beat any of the boys wrestling, or running a foot race, in pitching quoits, or tossing a copper - could ruin more liquor than all the boys of the town together, and the dignity and impartiality with which he presided at a horse race or fist fight excited the admiration and won the praise of everybody that was present and participated. I sympathized with him because he was struggling with difficulties, and so was I. Mr. Lincoln served with me in the Legislature in 1836 when we both retired, and he subsided, or became submerged, and was lost sight of as a public man for some years.

In 1846, when Wilmot introduced his celebrated proviso, and the Abolition tornado swept over the country, Lincoln again turned up as a member of Congress from the Sangamon district. I was then in the Senate of the United States, and was glad to welcome my old friend and companion. While in Congress, he distinguished himself by his opposition to the Mexican War, taking the side of the common enemy against his own country; and when he returned home, he found that the indignation of the people followed him everywhere, and he was again submerged or obliged to retire into private life, forgotten by his former friends. He came up again in 1854, just in time to make an Abolition or Black Republican platform, in company with Giddings, Lovejoy, Chase, and Fred Douglass, for the Republican party to stand upon.

These two men, having formed this combination to abolitionize the old Whig party and the old Democratic party,
and put themselves into the Senate of the United States, in
pursuance of their bargain, are now carrying out that arrangement. Matheny states that Trumbull broke faith - that
the bargain was that Lincoln should be the Senator in
Shield's place, and Trumbull cheated Lincoln, having control of four or five abolitionized Democrats who were
holding over in the Senate; he would not let them vote for
Lincoln, which obliged the rest of the Abolitionists to support him in order to secure an Abolition Senator. There are
a number of authorities for the truth of this besides
Matheny, and I suppose that even Mr. Lincoln will not deny
it.

Washington, Jefferson, Franklin, Hamilton, Jay, and the
great men of that day made this government divided into
free States and slave States, and left each State perfectly free
to do as it pleased on the subject of slavery. Why can it not
exist on the same principles on which our fathers made it?
They knew when they framed the Constitution that in a
country as wide and broad as this, with such a variety of
climate, production, and interest, the people necessarily required different laws and regulations; what would suit the
granite hills of New Hampshire would be unsuited to the
rice plantations of South Carolina, and they therefore provided that each State should retain its own Legislature and
its own sovereignty, with the full and complete power to do
as it pleased within its own limits, in all that was local and
not national.

One of the reserved rights of the States was the right to
regulate the relations between master and servant on the
slavery question. At the time the Constitution was framed,
there were thirteen States in the Union, twelve of which

were slaveholding States and one a free State. Suppose this doctrine of uniformity preached by Mr. Lincoln - that the States should all be free or all be slave - had prevailed. What would have been the result? Of course, the twelve slaveholding States would have overruled the one free State, and slavery would have fastened by a Constitutional provision on every inch of the American Republic, instead of being left, as our fathers wisely left it, to each State to decide for itself. Here I assert that uniformity in the local laws and institutions of the different States is neither possible nor desirable. If uniformity had been adopted when the government was established, it must inevitably have been the uniformity of slavery everywhere, or else the uniformity of negro citizenship and negro equality everywhere.

We are told by Lincoln that he is utterly opposed to the Dred Scott decision, and will not submit to it, for the reason that he says it deprives the negro of the rights and privileges of citizenship. That is the first and main reason which he assigns for his warfare on the Supreme Court of the United States and its decision. I ask you, are you in favor of conferring upon a negro the rights and privileges of citizenship? Do you desire to strike out of our State Constitution that clause which keeps savages and free negroes out of the State, and allow the free negroes to flow in, and cover your prairies with black settlements? Do you desire to turn this beautiful State into a free negro colony, in order that when Missouri abolishes slavery she can send one hundred thousand emancipated slaves into Illinois, to become citizens and voters, on an equality with yourselves? If you desire negro citizenship, if you desire to allow them to come into the State and settle with the white man, if you desire them to vote on an equality with yourselves, and to make them eligible to office, to serve on juries, and to adjudge your rights - then support Mr. Lincoln and the Black

Republican party, who are in favor of the citizenship of the negro. For one, I am opposed to negro citizenship in any and every form. I believe this government was made on the white basis. I believe it was made by white men for the benefit of white men and their posterity for ever; and I am in favor of confining citizenship to white men, men of European birth and descent, instead of conferring it upon negroes, Indians, and other inferior races.

Mr. Lincoln, following the example and lead of all the little Abolition orators who go around and lecture in the basements of schools and churches, reads from the Declaration of Independence that all men were created equal, and then asks how can you deprive a negro of that equality which God and the Declaration of Independence award to him? He and they maintain that negro equality is guaranteed by the laws of God, and that it is asserted in the Declaration of Independence. If they think so, of course they have a right to say so, and so vote. I do not question Mr. Lincoln's conscientious belief that the negro was made his equal, and hence is his brother; but for my own part, I do not regard the negro as my equal, and positively deny that he is my brother or any kin to me whatever. Lincoln has evidently learned by heart Parson Lovejoy's catechism. He can repeat it as well as Farnsworth, and he is worthy of a medal from Father Giddings and Fred Douglass for his Abolitionism. He holds that the negro was born his equal and yours, and that he was endowed with equality by the Almighty, and that no human law can deprive him of these rights which were guaranteed to him by the Supreme Ruler of the universe.

Now, I do not believe that the Almighty ever intended the negro to be the equal of the white man. If He did, He has been a long time demonstrating the fact. For thousands of years, the negro has been a race upon the earth, and during all that time, in all latitudes and climates, wherever he has wandered or been taken, he has been inferior to the race which he has there met. He belongs to an inferior race, and must always occupy an inferior position. I do not hold that because the negro is our inferior therefore he ought to be a slave. By no means can such a conclusion be drawn from what I have said. On the contrary, I hold that humanity and Christianity both require that the negro shall have and enjoy every right, every privilege, and every immunity consistent with the safety of the society in which he lives. On that point, I presume there can be no diversity of opinion. You and I are bound to extend to our inferior and dependent beings every right, every privilege, every faculty and immunity consistent with the public good.

The question then arises, what rights and privileges are consistent with the public good? This is a question which each State and each Territory must decide for itself - Illinois has decided it for herself. We have provided that the negro shall not be a slave, and we have also provided that he shall not be a citizen, but we protect him in his civil rights, in his life, his person and his property, only depriving him of all political rights whatsoever, and refusing to put him on an equality with the white man. That policy of Illinois is satisfactory to the Democratic party and to me, and if it were to the Republicans, there would then be no question upon the subject; but the Republicans say that he ought to be made a citizen, and when he becomes a citizen he becomes your equal, with all your rights and privileges. They assert the Dred Scott decision to be monstrous because it denies that the negro is or can be a citizen under the Constitution.

Now, I hold that Illinois had a right to abolish and prohibit slavery as she did, and I hold that Kentucky has the same right to continue and protect slavery that Illinois had to abolish it. I hold that New York had as much right to abolish slavery as Virginia has to continue it, and that each and every State of this Union is a sovereign power, with the right to do as it pleases upon the question of slavery, and upon all its domestic institutions. Slavery is not the only question which comes up in this controversy. There is a far more important one to you, and that is - what shall be done with the free negro? We have settled the slavery question as far as we are concerned; we have prohibited it in Illinois forever, and in doing so I think we have done wisely, and there is no man in the State who would be more strenuous in his opposition to the introduction of slavery than I would; but when we settled it for ourselves, we exhausted all our power over that subject. We have done our whole duty, and can do no more. We must leave each and every other State to decide for itself the same question.

In relation to the policy to be pursued toward the free negroes, we have said that they shall not vote, while Maine, on the other hand, has said that they shall vote. Maine is a sovereign State, and has the power to regulate the qualifications of voters within her limits. I would never consent to confer the right of voting and of citizenship upon a negro, but still I am not going to quarrel with Maine for differing from me in opinion. Let Maine take care of her own negroes, and fix the qualifications of her own voters to suit herself, without interfering with Illinois, and Illinois will not interfere with Maine. So with the State of New York. She allows the negro to vote provided he owns two hundred and fifty dollars' worth of property, but not otherwise. While I would not make any distinction whatever between a negro who held property and the one who did not, yet if the sovereign State of New York chooses to make that distinction, it is her business and not mine, and I will not quarrel with her for it. She can do as she pleases on this question if she minds her own business, and we will do the same thing.

Now, my friends, if we will only act conscientiously and rigidly upon this great principle of popular sovereignty, which guarantees to each State and Territory the right to do as it pleases on all things, local and domestic, instead of Congress interfering, we will continue at peace one with another. Why should Illinois be at war with Missouri, or Kentucky with Ohio, or Virginia with New York, merely because their institutions differ? They knew that the North and the South, having different climates, productions, and interests, required different institutions. This doctrine of Mr. Lincoln of uniformity among the institutions of the different States, is a new doctrine, never dreamed of by Washington, Madison, or the framers of this government. Mr. Lincoln and the Republican party set themselves up as wiser than these men who made this government, which has flourished for seventy years under the principle of popular sovereignty, recognizing the right of each State to do as it pleased.

Under that principle we have grown from a nation of three or four millions to a nation of about thirty millions of people; we have crossed the Alleghany Mountains and filled up the whole Northwest, turning the prairies into a garden, and building up churches and schools, thus spreading civilization and Christianity where before there was nothing but savage barbarism. Under that principle we have become, from a feeble nation, the most powerful on the face of the earth, and if we only adhere to that principle, we can go forward increasing in territory, in power, in strength, and in glory until the Republic of America shall be the north star that shall guide the friends of freedom throughout the civilized world. And why can we not adhere to the great principle of self-government upon which our institutions were originally based? I believe that this new doctrine preached by Mr. Lincoln and his party will dissolve the Union if it succeeds.

Afterward

Stephen Douglas defeated Abraham Lincoln in the 1858 Illinois Senate race but *The Lincoln-Douglas Debates* gained a national reputation for Lincoln. Lincoln received the 1860 Republican Party Presidential nomination. Douglas received the 1860 Democratic Party Presidential nomination. Lincoln defeated Douglas.

Stephen Douglas died on July 3, 1861.

Selected Reading

Capers, Gerald M., *Stephen A. Douglas, Defender of the Union*, 1959.

Carr, Clark E., *Stephen A. Douglas: His Life, Public Services, Speeches and Patriotism*, 1909.

Flint, Henry M., *Life of Stephen A. Douglas*, 1865.

Gardner, William, *Life of Stephen A. Douglas*, 1905.

Howland, Louis, *Stephen A. Douglas*, 1920.

Johannsen, Robert W., *Stephen A. Douglas*, 1973.

Johnson, Allen, *Stephen A. Douglas: A Study in American Politics*, 1970.

Sheahan, James W., *The Life of Stephen A. Douglas*, 1860.

Willis, Henry P., *Stephen A. Douglas*, 1910.

Frederick Douglass
The Great Sin and Shame Of America
July 5, 1852

I am not only an American slave but a man, and as such am bound to use my powers for the welfare of the whole human brotherhood.
- Frederick Douglass, February 26, 1846

In the early 1800's nearly 3,000,000 Americans were slaves. Frederick Augustus Washington Bailey - the son of a black slave, Harriet Bailey, and an unknown white father - was born in February 1817 on a Maryland plantation. In 1838, after years of physical abuse at the hands of slaveholders - *My diploma*, he would later say, *is written on my back.* - he escaped to the North on the Underground Railroad. Even in the North a fugitive slave was still legally property and subject to return to his *rightful owner.* To protect his new-found freedom, he used the name Frederick Douglass.

He spoke with personal knowledge and great power against slavery on behalf of the American Anti-Slavery Society, and audiences listened to him with rapt attention. Called because of his eloquence on their behalf *The Voice of the Colored People,* Douglass spent his life speaking, writing, and agitating against American slavery - March 12, 1839 - *We are American citizens, born with natural, inherent, and just rights!* - November 12, 1840 - *You degrade us and then ask why we are degraded; you shut our mouths, and then ask why we don't speak.* - December 23, 1845 - *The slaveholder is a not only a thief of men but a murderer of the soul.* - February 26, 1846 - *Have not I as good a right to be free as you have?* - May 12, 1846 - *A slave aspires to be his own master.* - March 30, 1849 - *Who is to decide which color is most pleasing to God?*

On July 5, 1854, in Rochester, New York's Corinthian Hall, Frederick Douglass delivered this landmark speech, *The Great Sin and Shame of America.*

Frederick Douglass

Fellow citizens, pardon me, and allow me to ask, why am I called upon to speak here today? What have I, or those I represent, to do with your national independence? Are the great principles of political freedom and of natural justice embodied in that Declaration of Independence extended to us? And am I, therefore, called upon to bring our humble offering to the national altar, and to confess the benefits, and express devout gratitude for the blessings, resulting from your independence to us?

Would to God, both for your sakes and ours, that an affirmative answer could be truthfully returned to these questions! Then would my task be light, and my burden easy and delightful. For who is there so cold that a nation's sympathy could not warm him? Who so obdurate and dead to the claims of gratitude that would not thankfully acknowledge such priceless benefits? Who so stolid and selfish that would not give his voice to swell the hallelujahs of a nation's jubilee, when the chains of servitude had been torn from his limbs? I am not that man. In a case like that, the dumb might eloquently speak, and the "lame man leap[s] as [a] hart."

But such is not the state of the case. I say it with a sad sense of the disparity between us. I am not included within the pale of this glorious anniversary! Your high independence only reveals the immeasurable distance between us. The blessings in which you this day rejoice are not enjoyed in common. The rich inheritance of justice, liberty, prosperity, and independence, bequeathed by your fathers, is shared by you, not by me. The sunlight that brought life and healing to you has brought stripes and death to me. This Fourth of July is yours, not mine. You may rejoice; I must mourn. To drag a man in fetters into the grand illuminated temple of liberty, and call upon him to join you in joyous anthems, were inhuman mockery and sacrilegious irony. Do you mean, citizens, to mock me, by asking me to speak today? If so, there is a parallel to your conduct. And let me warn you that it is dangerous to copy the example of a nation whose crimes, towering up to heaven, were thrown down by the breath of the Almighty, burying that nation in irrecoverable ruin! I can today take up the plaintive lament of a peeled and woe-smitten people.

> *By the rivers of Babylon, there we sat down. Yea! we wept when we remembered Zion. We hanged our harps upon the willows in the midst thereof. For there, they that carried us away captive, required of us a song; and they who wasted us required of us mirth, saying, "Sing us one of the songs of Zion." How can we sing the Lord's song in a strange land? If I forget thee, O Jerusalem, let my right hand forget her cunning. If I do not remember thee, let my tongue cleave to the roof of my mouth.*

Fellow citizens, above your national, tumultuous joy, I hear the mournful wail of millions, whose chains, heavy and grievous yesterday, are today rendered more intolerable by the jubilant shouts that reach them. If I do forget, if I do not faithfully remember those bleeding children of sorrow this day, *may my right hand forget her cunning, and may my tongue cleave to the roof of my mouth!* To forget them, to pass lightly over their wrongs, and to chime in with the popular theme, would be treason most scandalous and shocking, and would make me a reproach before God and the world. My subject, then, fellow-citizens, is American slavery. I shall see this day and its popular characteristics from the slave's point of view. Standing there, identified with the American bondman, making his wrongs mine, I do not hesitate to declare, with all my soul, that the character and conduct of this nation never looked blacker to me than on this Fourth of July. Whether we turn to the declarations of the past, or to the professions of the present, the conduct of the nation seems equally hideous and revolting. America is false to the past, false to the present, and solemnly binds herself to be false to the future. Standing with God and the crushed and bleeding slave on this occasion, I will, in the name of humanity which is outraged, in the name of liberty which is fettered, in the name of the Constitution and the Bible, which are disregarded and trampled upon, dare to call in question and to denounce, with all the emphasis I can command, everything that serves to perpetuate slavery - the great sin and shame of America! *I will not equivocate; I will not excuse;* I will use the severest language I can command; and yet not one word shall escape me that any man, whose judgment is not blinded by prejudice, or who is not at heart a slave-holder, shall not confess to be right and just.

But I fancy I hear someone of my audience say,

It is just in this circumstance that you and your brother abolitionists fail to make a favorable impression on the public mind. Would you argue more, and denounce less, would you persuade more and rebuke less, your cause would be much more likely to succeed.

But, I submit, where all is plain, there is nothing to be argued. What point in the antislavery creed would you have me argue? On what branch of the subject do the people of this country need light? Must I undertake to prove that the slave is a man? That point is conceded already. Nobody doubts it. The slave-holders themselves acknowledge it in the enactment of laws for their government. They acknowledge it when they punish disobedience on the part of the slave. There are seventy-two crimes in the state of Virginia, which, if committed by a black man (no matter how ignorant he be), subject him to the punishment of death, while only two of these same crimes will subject a white man to the like punishment. What is this but the acknowledgment that the slave is a moral, intellectual, and responsible being? The manhood of the slave is conceded. It is admitted in the fact that Southern statute books are covered with enactments forbidding, under severe fines and penalties, the teaching of the slave to read or write. When you can point to any such laws, in reference to the beasts of the field, then I may consent to argue the manhood of the slave. When the dogs in your streets, when the fowls of the air, when the cattle on your hills, when the fish of the sea, and the reptiles that crawl, shall be unable to distinguish the slave from a brute, then will I argue with you that the slave is a man!

For the present, it is enough to affirm the equal manhood of the Negro race. Is it not astonishing that, while we are plowing, planting, and reaping, using all kinds of mechanical tools, erecting houses, constructing bridges, building ships, working in metals of brass, iron, copper, silver, and gold - that, while we are reading, writing, and ciphering, acting as clerks, merchants, and secretaries, having among us lawyers, doctors, ministers, poets, authors, editors, orators, and teachers - that, while we are engaged in all manner of enterprises common to other men - digging gold in California, capturing the whale in the Pacific, feeding sheep and cattle on the hillside, living, moving, acting, thinking, planning, living in families as husbands, wives, and children, and, above all, confessing and worshipping the Christian's God, and looking hopefully for life and immortality beyond the grave - we are called upon to prove that we are men!

Would you have me argue that man is entitled to liberty? That he is the rightful owner of his own body? You have already declared it. Must I argue the wrongfulness of slavery? Is that a question for Republicans? Is it to be settled by the rules of logic and argumentation, as a matter beset with great difficulty, involving a doubtful application of the principle of justice, hard to be understood? How should I look today in the presence of Americans, dividing and subdividing a discourse, to show that men have a natural right to freedom, speaking of it relatively and positively, negatively and affirmatively? To do so would be to make myself ridiculous and to offer an insult to your understanding. There is not a man beneath the canopy of heaven that does not know that slavery is wrong for him.

What? Am I to argue that it is wrong to make men brutes, to rob them of their liberty, to work them without wages, to keep them ignorant of their relations to their fellowmen, to beat them with sticks, to flay their flesh with the lash, to load their limbs with irons, to hunt them with dogs, to sell them at auction, to sunder their families, to knock out their teeth, to burn their flesh, to starve them into obedience and submission to their masters? Must I argue that a system, thus marked with blood and stained with pollution, is wrong? No, I will not. I have better employment for my time and strength than such arguments would imply.

What, then, remains to be argued? Is it that slavery is not divine - that God did not establish it - that our doctors of divinity are mistaken? There is blasphemy in the thought. That which is inhuman cannot be divine. Who can reason on such a proposition? They that can, may; I cannot. The time for such argument is past.

At a time like this, scorching irony, not convincing argument, is needed. Oh! Had I the ability, and could I reach the nation's ear, I would today pour out a fiery stream of biting ridicule, blasting reproach, withering sarcasm, and stern rebuke. For it is not light that is needed, but fire - it is not the gentle shower, but thunder. We need the storm, the whirlwind, and the earthquake. The feeling of the nation must be quickened - the conscience of the nation must be roused - the propriety of the nation must be startled - the hypocrisy of the nation must be exposed - and its crimes against God and man must be proclaimed and denounced.

What to the American slave is your Fourth of July? I answer - a day that reveals to him, more than all other days in the year, the gross injustice and cruelty to which he is the constant victim. To him, your celebration is a sham - your boasted liberty, an unholy license - your national greatness, swelling vanity - your sounds of rejoicing are empty and heartless - your denunciations of tyrants, brass-fronted impudence - your shouts of liberty and equality, hollow mockery - your prayers and hymns, your sermons and thanksgivings, with all your religious parade and solemnity, are to him mere bombast, fraud, deception, impiety, and hypocrisy, a thin veil to cover up crimes which would disgrace a nation of savages. There is not a nation on the earth guilty of practices more shocking and bloody than are the people of these United States at this very hour.

Go where you may, search where you will, roam through all the monarchies and despotisms of the old world, travel through South America, search out every abuse, and when you have found the last, lay your facts by the side of the everyday practices of this nation, and you will say with me that, for revolting barbarity and shameless hypocrisy, America reigns without a rival.

Take the American slave trade which, we are told by the papers, is especially prosperous just now. Ex-senator Benton tells us that the price of men was never higher than now. He mentions the fact to show that slavery is in no danger. This trade is one of the peculiarities of American institutions. It is carried on in all the large towns and cities in one-half of this confederacy; and millions are pocketed every year by dealers in this horrid traffic. In several states this trade is a chief source of wealth. It is called (in contradistinction to the foreign slave trade) *the internal slave trade*. It is probably called so too in order to divert from it the horror with which the foreign slave trade is contemplated. That trade has long since been denounced by this government as piracy. It has been denounced with burning words, from the high places of the nation, as an execrable traffic. To arrest it, to put an end to it, this nation keeps a squadron, at immense cost, on the coast of Africa. Everywhere in this country, it is safe to speak of this foreign slave trade as a most inhuman traffic, opposed alike to the laws of God and of man. The duty to extirpate and destroy it is admitted even by our doctors of divinity. In order to put an end to it, some of these last have consented that their colored brethren (nominally free) should leave this country, and establish themselves on the western coast of Africa. It is, however, a notable fact that, while so much execration is poured out by Americans upon those engaged in the foreign slave trade, the men engaged in the slave trade between the states pass without condemnation, and their business is deemed honorable.

Behold the practical operation of this internal slave trade - the American slave trade sustained by American politics and American religion! Here you will see men and women reared like swine for the market. You know what is a swine-drover? I will show you a man-drover. They inhabit all our Southern States. They perambulate the country, and crowd the highways of the nation with droves of human stock. You will see one of these human flesh jobbers, armed with pistol, whip, and bowie knife, driving a company of a hundred men, women, and children, from the Potomac to the slave market at New Orleans. Those wretched people are to be sold singly, or in lots, to suit purchasers. They are food for the cotton field and the deadly sugar mill. Mark the sad procession as it moves wearily along, and the inhuman wretch who drives them. Hear his savage yells and his blood-chilling oaths, as he hurries on his affrighted captives. There, see the old man, with locks thinned and gray. Cast one glance, if you please, upon that young mother, whose shoulders are bare to the scorching sun, her briny tears falling on the brow of the babe in her arms. See, too, that girl of thirteen, weeping - yes, weeping - as she thinks of the mother from whom she has been torn. The drove moves tardily. Heat and sorrow have nearly consumed their strength. Suddenly you hear a quick snap, like the discharge of a rifle - the fetters clank, and the chain rattles simultaneously - your ears are saluted with a scream that seems to have torn its way to the center of your soul. The crack you heard was the sound of the slave whip; the scream you heard was from the woman you saw with the babe. Her speed had faltered under the weight of her child and her chains - that gash on her shoulder tells her to move on. Follow this drove to New Orleans. Attend the auction; see men examined like horses; see the forms of women rudely and brutally exposed to the shocking gaze of American slave-buyers. See this drove sold and separated forever; and never forget the deep, sad sobs that arose from that scattered multitude. Tell me, citizens, where, under the sun, can you witness a spectacle more fiendish and shocking? Yet this is but a glance at the American slave trade, as it exists at this moment, in the ruling part of the United States.

I was born amid such sights and scenes. To me the American slave trade is a terrible reality. When a child, my soul was often pierced with a sense of its horrors. I lived on Philpot Street, Fell's Point, Baltimore, and have watched from the wharves the slave ships in the basin, anchored from the shore, with their cargoes of human flesh, waiting for favorable winds to waft them down the Chesapeake. There was, at that time, a grand slave mart kept at the head of Pratt Street, by Austin Woldfolk. His agents were sent into every town and county in Maryland, announcing their arrival through the papers, and on flaming hand-bills headed, *Cash for Negroes.* These men were generally well dressed and very captivating in their manners, ever ready to drink, to treat, and to gamble. The fate of many a slave has depended upon the turn of a single card; and many a child has been snatched from the arms of its mother by bargains arranged in a state of brutal drunkenness.

The flesh-mongers gather up their victims by dozens and drive them, chained, to the general depot at Baltimore. When a sufficient number have been collected here, a ship is chartered for the purpose of conveying the forlorn crew to Mobile or to New Orleans. From the slave-prison to the ship, they are usually driven in the darkness of night, for since the antislavery agitation a certain caution is observed.

In the deep, still darkness of midnight, I have been often aroused by the dead, heavy footsteps and the piteous cries of the chained gangs that passed our door. The anguish of my boyish heart was intense; and I was often consoled, when speaking to my mistress in the morning, to hear her say that the custom was very wicked - that she hated to hear the rattle of the chains, and the heart-rending cries. I was glad to find one who sympathized with me in my horror.

Fellow-citizens, this murderous traffic is today in active operation in this boasted republic. In the solitude of my spirit, I see clouds of dust raised on the highways of the South; I see the bleeding footsteps; I hear the doleful wail of fettered humanity, on the way to the slave markets, where the victims are to be sold like horses, sheep, and swine, knocked off to the highest bidder. There I see the tenderest ties ruthlessly broken, to gratify the lust, caprice, and rapacity of the buyers and sellers of men. My soul sickens at the sight.

Frederick Douglass

Is this the land your fathers loved?
The freedom which they toiled to win?
Is this the earth whereon they moved?
Are these the graves they slumber in?

But a still more inhuman, disgraceful, and scandalous state of things remains to be presented. By an act of the American Congress, not yet two years old, slavery has been nationalized in its most horrible and revolting form. By that act, Mason and Dixon's line has been obliterated; New York has become as Virginia; and the power to hold, hunt, and sell men, women, and children as slaves remains no longer a mere state institution, but is now an institution of the whole United States. The power is coextensive with the Star Spangled Banner and American Christianity. Where these go may also go the merciless slave-hunter. Where these are man is not sacred. He is a bird for the sportsman's gun. By that most foul and fiendish of all human decrees, the liberty and person of every man are put in peril. Your broad republican domain is a hunting-ground for men. Not for thieves and robbers, enemies of society, merely, but for men guilty of no crime. Your law-makers have commanded all good citizens to engage in this hellish sport. Your President, your Secretary of State, your lords, nobles, and ecclesiastics, enforce as a duty you owe to your free and glorious country and to your God, that you do this accursed thing. Not fewer than forty Americans have within the past two years been hunted down, and without a moment's warning, hurried away in chains, and consigned to slavery and excruciating torture. Some of these have had wives and children dependent on them for bread; but of this no account was made. The right of the hunter to his prey stands superior to the right of marriage, and to all rights in this republic, the rights of God included! For black men there are neither law, justice, humanity, nor religion. The fugitive slave law makes mercy to them a crime, and bribes the judge who tries them. An American judge gets ten dollars for every victim he consigns to slavery, and five when he fails to do so. The oath of any two villains is sufficient, under this hell-black enactment, to send the most pious and exemplary black man into the remorseless jaws of slavery! His own testimony is nothing. He can bring no witnesses for himself. The minister of American justice is bound by the law to hear but one side, and that side is the side of the oppressor. Let this damning fact be perpetually told. Let it be thundered around the world that, in tyrant-killing, king-hating, people-loving, democratic, Christian America, the seats of justice are filled with judges who hold their office under an open and palpable bribe, and are bound in deciding in the case of a man's liberty to hear only his accusers!

In glaring violation of justice, in shameless disregard of the forms of administering law, in cunning arrangement to entrap the defenseless, and in diabolical intent, this fugitive slave law stands alone in the annals of tyrannical legislation. I doubt if there be another nation on the globe having the brass and the baseness to put such a law on the statute-book. If any man in this assembly thinks differently from me in this matter, and feels able to disprove my statements, I will gladly confront him at any suitable time and place he may select.

Afterward

In 1845 Frederick Douglass published his autobiography, *Narrative of the Life of Frederick Douglass, an American Slave, Written by Himself,* and with the proceeds he purchased his own freedom for $710.96.

Frederick Douglass died on February 20, 1895.

Frederick Douglass

Selected Reading

Douglass, Frederick, *Narrative of the Life of Frederick Douglass, an American Slave, Written by Himself*, 1845.

_____, *My Bondage and My Freedom*, 1855.

_____, *The Life and Times of Frederick Douglass*, 1881.

Foner, Philip, *Frederick Douglass*, 1964.

McFeely, William, *Frederick Douglass*, 1991.

Ralph Waldo Emerson
The American Scholar
August 31, 1837

America's intellectual Declaration of Independence.
- Oliver Wendell Holmes, Sr.

An event without any parallel in American literary history.
- James Russell Lowell

Ralph Waldo Emerson was born on May 25, 1803 in Boston, Massachusetts, the son of William and Ruth (Haskins) Emerson. Receiving his formal education at Harvard College and Harvard Divinity School, Emerson went on to serve as junior pastor of Boston's Second Church. On a year-long sabbatical to study in Europe, Emerson immersed himself in the philosophical writings of Locke, Kant, and Hegel, whose influence led him to a lifelong belief in transcendentalism.

Upon his return, Emerson published his first book, *Nature*, a transcendentalist view of the natural world. Emerson also began to give weekly lectures on transcendentalism at Boston's Masonic Temple on topics such as *The Philosophy of History* and *The Humanity of Science*. Emerson's well-attended lectures gained him a reputation as a brilliant speaker.

On June 22, 1837, Harvard's Phi Beta Kappa Society invited Emerson to give the lecture at its annual meeting. The two hundred invited guests, *the most distinguished that could be gathered in America,* included President John Quincy Adams, Senator Daniel Webster, U.S. Supreme Court Justice Joseph Story, Dr. Oliver Wendell Holmes, Sr., James Russell Lowell, and Henry David Thoreau.

On August 31, 1837, at Cambridge's First Parish Church, Ralph Waldo Emerson delivered a call for American literary independence in this landmark speech, *The American Scholar.*

The next great influence into the spirit of the scholar is the mind of the past, in whatever form, whether of literature, of art, of institutions, that mind is inscribed. Books are the best type of the influence of the past, and perhaps we shall get at the truth - learn the amount of this influence more conveniently - by considering their value alone.

The theory of books is noble. The scholar of the first age received into him the world around, brooded thereon, gave it the new arrangement of his own mind, and uttered it again. It came into him life; it went out from him truth. It came to him short-lived actions; it went out from him immortal thoughts. It came to him business; it went from him poetry. It was dead fact; now, it is quick thought. It can stand, and it can go. It now endures, it now flies, it now inspires. Precisely in proportion to the depth of mind from which it issued, so high does it soar, so long does it sing.

Or, I might say, it depends on how far the process had gone, of transmuting life into truth. In proportion to the completeness of the distillation, so will the purity and imperishableness of the product be. But none is quite perfect. As no air-pump can by any means make a perfect vacuum, so neither can any artist entirely exclude the conventional, the local, the perishable from his book, or write a book of pure thought, that shall be as efficient, in all respects, to a remote posterity, as to contemporaries, or rather to the second age. Each age, it is found, must write its own books, or rather, each generation for the next succeeding. The books of an older period will not fit this.

Yet hence arises a grave mischief. The sacredness which attaches to the act of creation, the act of thought, is transferred to the record. The poet chanting was felt to be a divine man - henceforth the chant is divine also. The writer was a just and wise spirit - henceforward it is settled the book is perfect, as love of the hero corrupts into worship of his statue. Instantly the book becomes noxious - the guide is a tyrant. The sluggish and perverted mind of the multitude, slow to open to the incursions of reason, having once so opened, having once received this book, stands upon it, and makes an outcry if it is disparaged. Colleges are built on it. Books are written on it by thinkers, not by man thinking - by men of talent, that is, who start wrong, who set out from accepted dogmas, not from their own sight of principles. Meek young men grow up in libraries, believing it their duty to accept the views which Cicero, which Locke, which Bacon, have given, forgetful that Cicero, Locke, and Bacon were only young men in libraries when they wrote these books.

Hence, instead of man thinking, we have the bookworm. Hence the book-learned class, who value books, as such - not as related to nature and the human constitution, but as making a sort of third estate with the world and the soul. Hence the restorers of readings, the emendators, the bibliomaniacs of all degrees.

Books are the best of things, well used - abused, among the worst. What is the right use? What is the one end which all means go to effect? They are for nothing but to inspire. I had better never see a book than to be warped by its attraction clean out of my own orbit, and made a satellite instead of a system. The one thing in the world of value is the active soul. This every man is entitled to; this every man contains within him, although in almost all men obstructed and as yet unborn. The soul active sees absolute truth and utters truth, or creates. In this action it is genius, not the privilege of here and there a favorite, but the sound estate of every man. In its essence it is progressive. The book, the college, the school of art, the institution of any kind, stop with some past utterance of genius. This is good, say they, let us hold by this. They pin me down. They look backward and not forward. But genius looks forward - the eyes of man are set in his forehead, not in his hindhead; man hopes, genius creates. Whatever talents may be, if the man create not, the pure efflux of the Deity is not his; cinders and smoke there may be, but not yet flame. There are creative manners, there are creative actions, and creative words - manners, actions, words, that is, indicative of no custom or authority, but springing spontaneous from the mind's own sense of good and fair.

On the other part, instead of being its own seer, let it receive from another mind its truth, though it were in torrents of light, without periods of solitude, inquest, and self-recovery, and a fatal disservice is done. Genius is always sufficiently the enemy of genius by over-influence. The literature of every nation bears me witness. The English dramatic poets have Shakespearized now for two hundred years.

Undoubtedly there is a right way of reading, so it be sternly subordinated. Man thinking must not be subdued by his instruments. Books are for the scholar's idle times. When he can read God directly, the hour is too precious to be wasted in other men's transcripts of their readings. But when the intervals of darkness come, as come they must, when the sun is hid and the stars withdraw their shining, we repair to the lamps which were kindled by their ray, to guide our steps to the East again, where the dawn is. We hear, that we may speak. The Arabian says, "A fig tree, looking on a fig tree, becometh fruitful."

It is remarkable, the character of the pleasure we derive from the best books. They impress us with the conviction that one nature wrote and the same reads. We read the verses of one of the great English poets, of Chaucer, of Marvell, of Dryden, with the most modern joy - with a pleasure, I mean, which is in great part caused by the abstraction of all time from their verses. There is some awe mixed with the joy of our surprise, when this poet, who lived in some past world, two or three hundred years ago, says that which lies close to my own soul, that which I also had well-nigh thought and said. But for the evidence thence afforded to the philosophical doctrine of the identity of all minds, we should suppose some preestablished harmony, some foresight of souls that were to be, and some preparation of stores for their future wants, like the fact observed in insects, who lay up food before death for the young grub they shall never see.

I would not be hurried by any love of system, by any exaggeration of instincts, to underrate the book. We all know that as the human body can be nourished on any food, though it were boiled grass and the broth of shoes, so the human mind can be fed by any knowledge. And great and heroic men have existed who had almost no other information than by the printed page. I only would say that it needs a strong head to bear that diet. One must be an inventor to read well. As the proverb says, *He that would bring home the wealth of the Indies must carry out the wealth of the Indies.* There is then creative reading as well as creative writing. When the mind is braced by labor and invention, the page of whatever book we read becomes luminous with manifold allusion. Every sentence is doubly significant, and the sense of our author is as broad as the world. We then see what is always true - that as the seer's hour of vision is short and rare among heavy days and months, so is its record, perchance, the least part of his volume. The discerning will read, in his Plato or Shakespeare, only that least part, only the authentic utterances of the oracle; all the rest he rejects, were it never so many times Plato's and Shakespeare's.

Of course there is a portion of reading quite indispensable to a wise man. History and exact science he must learn by laborious reading. Colleges, in like manner, have their indispensable office, to teach elements. But they can only highly serve us when they aim not to drill, but to create - when they gather from far every ray of various genius to their hospitable halls and, by the concentrated fires, set the hearts of their youth on flame. Thought and knowledge are natures in which apparatus and pretension avail nothing. Gowns and pecuniary foundations, though of towns of gold, can never countervail the least sentence or syllable of wit. Forget this, and our American colleges will recede in their public importance, whilst they grow richer every year.

Afterward

The American Scholar established Emerson as a leading lecturer, and two literary works - *Essays* (1841) and *Essays: Second Series* (1844) - established him as a leading writer. The Transcendental Movement which he led grew in importance throughout his life.

Ralph Waldo Emerson on died April 27, 1822.

Selected Reading

Allen, Gay W., *Waldo Emerson: A Biography*, 1981.
Conway, Moncure D., *Emerson at Home and Abroad*, 1968.
Cooke, George W., *Ralph Waldo Emerson: His Life, Writings, and Philosophy*, 1971.
Garnett, Richard, *Life of Ralph Waldo Emerson*, 1974.
Snider, Denton J., *A Biography of Ralph Waldo Emerson*, 1977.

Samuel Gompers
The Eight-Hour Day
May 1, 1890

We are determined to have an eight-hour workday.
- Samuel Gompers' *Letter To The President* (1890)

America's industrial revolution was led by men like John D. Rockefeller and Henry Ford, who could organize production and manufacturing. America's labor revolution was led by Samuel Gompers, a man who could organize workers.

Samuel Gompers was born on January 27, 1850 in London, England, the son of Solomon and Sarah (Rood) Gompers. After the Gompers family immigrated to America in 1863, Sam went to work as a cigar maker in New York City. On November 24, 1875, Gompers was elected President of the United Cigar Workers, representing some 500 workers. In July 1877 his first successful strike prevented a threatened pay cut from $18 to $12 a week.

Samuel Gompers founded the American Federation of Labor - a union of unions - on December 8, 1886. Under his tireless, almost forty-year leadership, AFL membership grew to a quarter of a million by 1890, a million and a half by 1904, two million by 1917, and five million by 1924. In 1888 Samuel Gompers called on all AFL unions to demand, either by peaceful negotiation or painful strikes, an eight-hour workday. To build labor support for an eight-hour day, Gompers traveled across the country, speaking to workers. To build public and political support for an eight-hour day, Gompers planned four days of nationwide rallies to be held in over 240 American cities - Washington's Birthday, Labor Day, Independence Day, and May Day, 1890.

At New York City's May Day rally, Samuel Gompers delivered this landmark speech, *The Eight-Hour Day*.

My friends, we have met here today to celebrate the idea that has prompted thousands of working people of Louisville and New Albany to parade the streets of y[our city] - that prompts the toilers of Chicago to turn out by their fifty or hundred thousand of men - that prompts the vast army of wage workers in New York to demonstrate their enthusiasm and appreciation of the importance of this idea - that prompts the toilers of England, Ireland, Germany, France, Italy, Spain, and Austria to defy the manifestos of the autocrats of the world and say that on May the first, 1890, the wage workers of the world will lay down their tools in sympathy with the wage workers of America, to establish a principle of limitations of hours of labor to eight hours for sleep, eight hours for work, and eight hours for what we will.

It has been charged time and again that were we to have more hours of leisure we would merely devote it to debauchery, to the cultivation of vicious habits - in other words, that we would get drunk. I desire to say this in answer to that charge - as a rule, there are two classes in society who get drunk. One is the class who has no work to do in consequence of too much money, the other class, who also has no work to do, because it can't get any, and gets drunk on its face. I maintain that that class in our social life that exhibits the greatest degree of sobriety is that class who are able, by a fair number of hours of day's work to earn fair wages, not overworked. The man who works twelve, fourteen, and sixteen hours a day requires some artificial stimulant to restore the life ground out of him in the drudgery of the day.

We ought to be able to discuss this question on a higher ground, and I am pleased to say that the movement in which we are engaged will stimulate us to it. They tell us that the eight-hour movement cannot be enforced, for the reason that it must check industrial and commercial progress. I say that the history of this country, in its industrial and commercial relations, shows the reverse. I say that is the plane on which this question ought to be discussed; that is the social question. As long as they make this question an economic one, I am willing to discuss it with them. I would retrace every step I have taken to advance this movement did it mean industrial and commercial stagnation. But it does not mean that. It means greater prosperity; it means a greater degree of progress for the whole people; it means more advancement and intelligence, and a nobler race of people. . . .

They say they can't afford it. Is that true? Let us see for one moment. If a reduction in the hours of labor causes industrial and commercial ruination, it would naturally follow [that] increased hours of labor would increase the prosperity, commercial and industrial. If that were true, England and America ought to be at the tail end, and China at the head of civilization.

Is it not a fact that we find laborers in England and the United States, where the hours are eight, nine, and ten hours a day - do we not find that the employers and laborers are more successful? Don't we find them selling articles cheaper? We do not need to trust the modern moralist to tell us those things. In all industries where the hours of labor are long, there you will find the least development of the power of invention. Where the hours of labor are long, men are cheap, and where men are cheap there is no necessity for invention. How can you expect a man to work ten or twelve or fourteen hours at his calling and then devote any time to the invention of a machine or discovery of a new principle or force? If he be so fortunate as to be able to read a paper, he will fall asleep before he has read through the second or third line.

Why, when you reduce the hours of labor, say an hour a day, just think what it means. Suppose men who work ten hours a day had the time lessened to nine, or men who work nine hours a day have it reduced to eight hours - what does it mean? It means millions of golden hours and opportunities for thought. Some men might say you will go to sleep. Well, some men might sleep sixteen hours a day; the ordinary man might try that, but he would soon find he could not do it long. He would have to do something. He would probably go to the theater one night, to a concert another night, but he could not do that every night. He would probably become interested in some study and the hours that have been taken from manual labor are devoted to mental labor, and the mental labor of one hour will produce for him more wealth than the physical labor of a dozen hours.

I maintain that this is a true proposition, that men under the short-hour system not only have opportunity to improve themselves, but to make a greater degree of prosperity for their employers. Why, my friends, how is it in China, how is it in Spain, how is it in India and Russia, how is it in Italy? Cast your eye throughout the universe and observe the industry that forces nature to yield up its fruits to man's necessities, and you will find that where the hours of labor are the shortest the progress of invention in machinery and the prosperity of the people are the greatest. It is the greatest impediment to progress to hire men cheaply. Wherever men are cheap, there you find the least degree of progress. It has only been under the great influence of our great republic, where our people have exhibited their great senses, that we can move forward, upward and onward, and are watched with interest in our movements of progress and reform. . . .

The man who works the long hours has no necessities except the barest to keep body and soul together, so he can work. He goes to sleep and dreams of work; he rises in the morning to go to work; he takes his frugal lunch to work; he comes home again to throw himself down on a miserable apology for a bed so that he can get that little rest that he may be able to go to work again. He is nothing but a veritable machine. He lives to work instead of working to live.

My friends, the only thing the working people need, besides the necessities of life, is time. Time. Time with which our lives begin - time with which our lives close - time to cultivate the better nature within us - time to brighten our homes. Time, which brings us from the lowest condition up to the highest civilization - time, so that we can raise men to a higher plane.

My friends, you will find that it has been ascertained that there is more than a million of our brothers and sisters, able-bodied men and women, on the streets, and on the highways and byways of our country willing to work but who cannot find it. You know that it is the theory of our government that we can work or cease to work at will. It is only a theory. You know that it is only a theory and not a fact. It is true that we can cease to work when we want to, but I deny that we can work when we will, so long as there are a million idle men and women tramping the streets of our cities, searching for work. The theory that we can work or cease to work when we will is a delusion and a snare. It is a lie.

What we want to consider is, first, to make our employment more secure, and, secondly, to make wages more permanent, and, thirdly, to give these poor people a chance to work. The laborer has been regarded as a mere producing machine, . . . but back of labor is the soul of man and honesty of purpose and aspiration. Now you cannot, as the political economists and college professors, say that labor is a commodity to be bought and sold. I say we are American citizens with the heritage of all the great men who have stood before us, men who have sacrificed all in the cause except honor. Our enemies would like to see this movement thrust into Hades; they would like to see it in a warmer climate, but I say to you that this labor movement has come to stay. Like Banquo's ghost, it will not down. I say the labor movement is a fixed fact. It has grown out of the necessities of the people, and, although some may desire to see it fail, still the labor movement will be found to have a strong lodgment in the hearts of the people, and we will go on until success has been achieved.

We want eight hours and nothing less. We have been accused of being selfish, and it has been said that we will want more, that last year we got an advance of ten cents and now we want more. We do want more. You will find that a man generally wants more. Go and ask a tramp what he wants, and if he doesn't want a drink he will want a good, square meal. You ask a workingman, who is getting two dollars a day, and he will say that he wants ten cents more. Ask a man who gets five dollars a day and he will want fifty cents more. The man who receives five thousand dollars a year wants six thousand dollars a year, and the man who owns eight or nine hundred thousand dollars will want a hundred thousand dollars more to make it a million, while the man who has his millions will want everything he can lay his hands on and then raise his voice against the poor devil who wants ten cents more a day. We live in the latter part of the nineteenth century. In the age of electricity and steam that has produced wealth a hundred fold, we insist that it has been brought about by the intelligence and energy of the workingmen, and while we find that it is now easier to produce, it is harder to live. We do want more, and when it becomes more, we shall still want more. And we shall never cease to demand more until we have received the results of our labor.

Afterward

On Janaury 1, 1917, after a twenty-seven year struggle, President Woodrow Wilson signed into law the Adamson Act, which permanently established the eight-hour workday.

Samuel Gompers led the ALF-CIO until his death on December 13, 1924.

Selected Reading

Chasan, Will, *Samuel Gompers*, 1971.
Gompers, Samuel, *Seventy Years of Life and Labor*, 1925.
Harvey, Rowland, *Samuel Gompers*, 1971.
Mandel, Bernard, *Samuel Gompers*, 1963.

Andrew Jackson
Second Inaugural Address
March 4, 1833

The Union must be preserved. I will die for the Union.
- President Andrew Jackson, December 14, 1832

Andrew Jackson, Jr., *Old Hickory*, was born on March 15, 1767 in the Waxhaw Settlement, South Carolina, the child of Andrew and Elizabeth (Hutchinson) Jackson. At thirteen Jackson enlisted in the Revolutionary Army. After the War, he studied law and, in 1788, set up practice in Nashville, Tennessee. In 1796 he was elected to the U.S. House of Representatives and in 1797 to the U.S. Senate. In the War of 1812, President Madison commissioned Jackson (who had won fame in the Indian Wars) as a U.S. Army General. On January 1, 1815, General Jackson's forces defeated the British at the Battle of New Orleans. Jackson was elected President in 1828 and re-elected in 1832.

The most important event in the Jackson Presidency was the Nullification Crisis. On July 14, 1832, Jackson signed into law a protective tariff, which Southern opponents called the *Tariff of Abomination*. On November 24, 1832, South Carolina adopted a Nullification Ordinance, claiming a State right to declare Federal law null and void. On January 16, 1833, Jackson proposed to Congress the *Force Act*, giving the Federal Government the right to use military force to enforce the tariff. A compromise tariff to avert civil war was negotiated and signed on March 2, 1833.

On March 4, 1833, Inauguration Day, President Andrew Jackson signed into law the *Force Act*, affirming his intention to preserve the Union, if necessary by military force. He then delivered his landmark *Second Inaugural Address*.

Andrew Jackson

The will of the American people, expressed through their unsolicited suffrages, calls me before you to pass through the solemnities preparatory to taking upon myself the duties of President of the United States for another term. For their approbation of my public conduct through a period which has not been without its difficulties, and for this renewed expression of their confidence in my good intentions, I am at a loss for terms adequate to the expression of my gratitude.

It shall be displayed to the extent of my humble abilities in continued efforts so to administer the government as to preserve their liberty and promote their happiness.

So many events have occurred within the last four years which have necessarily called forth - sometimes under circumstances the most delicate and painful - my views of the principles and policy which ought to be pursued by the general government, that I need on this occasion but allude to a few leading considerations connected with some of them.

The foreign policy adopted by our government soon after the formation of our present Constitution, and very generally pursued by successive administrations, has been crowned with almost complete success, and has elevated our character among the nations of the earth. To do justice to all and to submit to wrong from none has been during my administration its growing maxim, and so happy have been its results that we are not only at peace with all the world, but have few causes of controversy, and those of minor importance, remaining unadjusted.

In the domestic policy of this government, there are two objects which especially deserve the attention of the people and their representatives, and which have been and will continue to be the subjects of my increasing solicitude. They are the preservation of the rights of the several States and the integrity of the Union.

These great objects are necessarily connected, and can only be attained by an enlightened exercise of the powers of each within its appropriate sphere, in conformity with the public will constitutionally expressed. To this end it becomes the duty of all to yield a ready and patriotic submission to the laws constitutionally enacted, and thereby promote and strengthen a proper confidence in those institutions of the several States and of the United States which the people themselves have ordained for their own government.

My experience in public concerns and the observation of a life somewhat advanced confirm the opinions long since imbibed by me, that the destruction of our State governments or the annihilation of their control over the local concerns of the people would lead directly to revolution and anarchy, and finally to despotism and military domination. In proportion, therefore, as the general government encroaches upon the rights of the States, in the same proportion does it impair its own power and detract from its ability to fulfill the purposes of its creation. Solemnly impressed with these considerations, my countrymen will ever find me ready to exercise my constitutional powers in arresting measures which may directly or indirectly encroach upon the rights of the States or tend to consolidate all political power in the general government. But of equal and, indeed, of incalculable importance is the union of these States, and the sacred duty of all to contribute to its preservation by a liberal support of the general government in the exercise of its just powers. You have been wisely admonished to *accustom yourselves to think and speak of the Union as the palladium of your political safety and prosperity, watching for its preservation with jealous anxiety, discountenancing whatever may suggest even a suspicion that it can, in any event, be abandoned, and indignantly frowning upon the first dawning of any attempt to alienate any portion of our country from the rest, or to enfeeble the sacred ties which now link together the various parts.* Without union our independence and liberty would never have been achieved; without union they never can be maintained. Divided into twenty-four, or even a smaller number, of separate communities, we shall see our internal trade burdened with numberless restraints and exactions, communication between distant points and sections obstructed or cut off, our sons made soldiers to deluge with blood the fields they now till in peace, the mass of our people borne down and impoverished by taxes to support armies and navies, and military leaders at the head of their victorious legions becoming our lawgivers and judges. The loss of liberty, of all good government, of peace, plenty, and happiness, must inevitably follow a dissolution of the Union. In supporting it, therefore, we support all that is dear to the freeman and the philanthropist.

The time at which I stand before you is full of interest. The eyes of all nations are fixed on our Republic. The event of the existing crisis will be decisive in the opinion of mankind of the practicability of our federal system of government. Great is the stake placed in our hands; great is the responsibility which must rest upon the people of the United States. Let us realize the importance of the attitude in which we stand before the world. Let us exercise forbearance and firmness. Let us extricate our country from the dangers which surround it, and learn wisdom from the lessons they inculcate.

Deeply impressed with the truth of these observations, and under the obligation of that solemn oath which I am about to take, I shall continue to exert all my faculties to maintain the just powers of the Constitution and to transmit unimpaired to posterity the blessings of our federal Union. At the same time it will be my aim to inculcate by my official acts the necessity of exercising by the general government those powers only that are clearly delegated, to encourage simplicity and economy in the expenditures of the government, to raise no more money from the people than may be requisite for these objects, and in a manner that will best promote the interests of all classes of the community and of all portions of the Union. Constantly bearing in mind that in entering into society *individuals must give up a share of liberty to preserve the rest*, it will be my desire so to discharge my duties as to foster with our brethren in all parts of the country a spirit of liberal concession and compromise and, by reconciling our fellow citizens to those partial sacrifices which they must unavoidably make for the preservation of a greater good, to recommend our invaluable government and Union to the confidence and affections of the American people.

Finally, it is my most fervent prayer to that Almighty Being before whom I now stand, and who has kept us in His hands from the infancy of our Republic to the present day, that He will so overrule all my intentions and actions and inspire the hearts of my fellow citizens that we may be preserved from dangers of all kinds and continue forever a united and happy people.

Andrew Jackson

Afterward

President Andrew Jackson's success in defusing the Nullification Crisis forestalled, but could not avert, a civil war.

Andrew Jackson died on June 8, 1845.

Selected Reading

Bassett, John S., *The Life of Andrew Jackson*, 1967.
Coit, Margaret L., *Andrew Jackson*, 1965.
Collier, Christopher, and James L. Collier, *Andrew Jackson's America*, 1999.
Davis, Burke, *Old Hickory: A Life of Andrew Jackson*, 1977.
Remini, Robert, *Andrew Jackson*, 1984.
Schlesinger, Arthur M., Jr., *The Age of Jackson*, 1953.
Ward, John W., *Andrew Jackson, Symbol for an Age*, 1955.

Fiction
Byrd, Max, *Jackson: A Novel*, 1997.

Thomas Jefferson
First Inaugural Address
March 4, 1801

We hold these truths to be sacred and undeniable, that all men are created equal and independent - that from that equal creation they derive rights inherent and inalienable, among which are the preservation of life, and liberty, and the pursuit of happiness.

- Jefferson's Draft of the Declaration of Independence

On February 17, 1800, Republican presidential candidate Thomas Jefferson defeated the Federalist incumbent John Adams. Of the first peaceful transfer of power between two American political parties, *The Revolution of 1800*, Jefferson said it was, *As real a Revolution as that of 1776. Not effected by the sword but by the peaceful the suffrage of the people.*

Thomas Jefferson was born at *Shadwell* plantation in Goochland (now Albemarle) County, Virginia on April 13, 1743, the son of Peter and Jane (Randolph) Jefferson. At age fourteen Jefferson inherited the thousand acre plantation and its slaves. Jefferson spent two years at the College of William and Mary and studied the law for five years. In 1769 he began building a second plantation, *Monticello.* While serving in Virginia's House of Burgesses, Jefferson came to national fame in 1774 upon the publication of *A Summary View of the Rights of British America.* He served as a delegate to the Second Continental Congress where he was selected to write the Declaration of Independence. Jefferson served as Virginia's Governor, in the Continental Congress, as Minister to France, as U.S. Secretary of State, and as Vice President.

On March 4, 1801, in the U.S. Senate Chamber, Thomas Jefferson took the oath as third President of the United States. He then delivered his landmark *First Inaugural Address.*

Friends and fellow citizens, called upon to undertake the duties of the First Executive office of our country, I avail myself of the presence of that portion of my fellow citizens which is here assembled to express my grateful thanks for the favor with which they have been pleased to look toward me, to declare a sincere consciousness that the task is above my talents, and that I approach it with those anxious and awful presentiments which the greatness of the charge and the weakness of my powers so justly inspire. A rising nation, spread over a wide and fruitful land, traversing all the seas with the rich productions of their industry, engaged in commerce with nations who feel power and forget right, advancing rapidly to destinies beyond the reach of mortal eye - when I contemplate these transcendent objects, and see the honor, the happiness, and the hopes of this beloved country committed to the issue and the auspices of this day, I shrink from the contemplation, and humble myself before the magnitude of the undertaking. Utterly, indeed, should I despair did not the presence of many whom I here see remind me that in the other high authorities provided by our Constitution I shall find resources of wisdom, of virtue, and of zeal on which to rely under all difficulties. To you, then, gentlemen, who are charged with the sovereign functions of legislation, and to those associated with you, I look with encouragement for that guidance and support which may enable us to steer with safety the vessel in which we are all embarked amidst the conflicting elements of a troubled world.

During the contest of opinion through which we have passed, the animation of discussions and of exertions has sometimes worn an aspect which might impose on strangers unused to think freely and to speak and to write what they think, but this being now decided by the voice of the nation, announced according to the rules of the Constitution, all will, of course, arrange themselves under the will of the law, and unite in common efforts for the common good. All, too, will bear in mind this sacred principle - that though the will of the majority is in all cases to prevail, that will to be rightful must be reasonable, that the minority possess their equal rights, which equal law must protect, and to violate would be oppression. Let us, then, fellow citizens, unite with one heart and one mind. Let us restore to social intercourse that harmony and affection without which liberty and even life itself are but dreary things. And let us reflect that, having banished from our land that religious intolerance under which mankind so long bled and suffered, we have yet gained little if we countenance a political intolerance as despotic, as wicked, and capable of as bitter and bloody persecutions. During the throes and convulsions of the ancient world, during the agonizing spasms of infuriated man, seeking through blood and slaughter his long-lost liberty, it was not wonderful that the agitation of the billows should reach even this distant and peaceful shore - that this should be more felt and feared by some and less by others, and should divide opinions as to measures of safety. But every difference of opinion is not a difference of principle. We have called by different names brethren of the same principle. We are all Republicans; we are all Federalists. If there be any among us who would wish to dissolve this Union or to change its republican form, let them stand undisturbed as monuments of the safety with which error of opinion may be tolerated where reason is left free to combat it. I know, indeed, that some honest men fear that a republican government cannot be strong, that this Government is not strong enough; but would the honest patriot, in the full tide of successful experiment, abandon a government which has so far kept us free and firm on the theoretic and visionary fear that this Government, the world's best hope, may by possibility want energy to preserve itself? I trust not. I believe this, on the contrary, the strongest Government on earth. I believe it the only one where every man, at the call of the law, would fly to the standard of the law, and would meet invasions of the public order as his own personal concern. Sometimes it is said that man cannot be trusted with the government of himself. Can he, then, be trusted with the government of others? Or have we found angels in the forms of kings to govern him? Let history answer this question.

Let us, then, with courage and confidence, pursue our own Federal and Republican principles, our attachment to union and representative government. Kindly separated by nature and a wide ocean from the exterminating havoc of one quarter of the globe - too high-minded to endure the degradations of the others - possessing a chosen country, with room enough for our descendants to the thousandth and thousandth generation - entertaining a due sense of our equal right to the use of our own faculties, to the acquisitions of our own industry, to honor and confidence from our fellow-citizens, resulting not from birth, but from our actions and their sense of them - enlightened by a benign religion, professed, indeed, and practiced in various forms, yet all of them inculcating honesty, truth, temperance, gratitude, and the love of man - acknowledging and adoring an overruling Providence, which by all its dispensations proves that it delights in the happiness of man here and his greater happiness hereafter with all these blessings - what more is necessary to make us a happy and a prosperous people? Still one thing more, fellow citizens - a wise and frugal government, which shall restrain men from injuring one another, shall leave them otherwise free to regulate their own pursuits of industry and improvement, and shall not take from the mouth of labor the bread it has earned. This is the sum of good government, and this is necessary to close the circle of our felicities.

About to enter, fellow citizens, on the exercise of duties which comprehend everything dear and valuable to you, it is proper you should understand what I deem the essential principles of our Government, and consequently those which ought to shape its administration. I will compress them within the narrowest compass they will bear, stating the general principle, but not all its limitations - equal and exact justice to all men, of whatever state or persuasion, religious or political; peace, commerce, and honest friendship with all nations, entangling alliances with none; the support of the State governments in all their rights, as the most competent administrations for our domestic concerns and the surest bulwarks against anti-republican tendencies; the preservation of the General Government in its whole constitutional vigor, as the sheet anchor of our peace at home and safety abroad; a jealous care of the right of election by the people - a mild and safe corrective of abuses which are lopped by the sword of revolution where peaceable remedies are unprovided; absolute acquiescence in the decisions of the majority, the vital principle of republics, from which is no appeal but to force, the vital principle and immediate parent of despotism; a well-disciplined militia, our best reliance in peace and for the first moments of war, till regulars may relieve them; the supremacy of the civil over the military authority; economy in the public expense, that labor may be lightly burdened; the honest payment of our debts and sacred preservation of the public faith; encouragement of agriculture, and of commerce as its handmaid; the diffusion of information and arraignment of all abuses at the bar of the public reason; freedom of religion, freedom of the press, and freedom of person under the protection of the habeas corpus, and trial by juries impartially selected. These principles form the bright constellation which has gone before us and guided our steps through an age of revolution and reformation. The wisdom of our sages and blood of our heroes have been devoted to their attainment. They should be the creed of our political faith, the text of civic instruction, the touchstone by which to try the services of those we trust; and should we wander from them in moments of error or of alarm, let us hasten to retrace our steps and to regain the road which alone leads to peace, liberty, and safety.

I repair, then, fellow citizens, to the post you have assigned me. With experience enough in subordinate offices to have seen the difficulties of this the greatest of all, I have learnt to expect that it will rarely fall to the lot of imperfect man to retire from this station with the reputation and the favor which bring him into it. Without pretensions to that high confidence you reposed in our first and greatest revolutionary character, whose preeminent services had entitled him to the first place in his country's love and destined for him the fairest page in the volume of faithful history, I ask so much confidence only as may give firmness and effect to the legal administration of your affairs. I shall often go wrong through defect of judgment. When right, I shall often be thought wrong by those whose positions will not command a view of the whole ground. I ask your indulgence for my own errors, which will never be intentional, and your support against the errors of others, who may condemn what they would not if seen in all its parts. The approbation implied by your suffrage is a great consolation to me for the past, and my future solicitude will be to retain the good opinion of those who have bestowed it in advance, to conciliate that of others by doing them all the good in my power, and to be instrumental to the happiness and freedom of all.

Relying, then, on the patronage of your good will, I advance with obedience to the work, ready to retire from it whenever you become sensible how much better choice it is in your power to make. And may that Infinite Power which rules the destinies of the universe lead our councils to what is best, and give them a favorable issue for your peace and prosperity.

Afterward

Jefferson served as U.S. President from 1801 to 1809. He died on July 4, 1826, the fiftieth anniversary of the signing of the Declaration of Independence.

Selected Reading

Cunningham, Noble E., Jr., *In Pursuit of Reason: The Life of Thomas Jefferson*, 1987.

Harrison, Maureen, and Steve Gilbert, Editors, *Thomas Jefferson: Word for Word*, 1993.

Johnstone, Robert M., Jr., *Jefferson and the Presidency: Leadership in the Young Republic*, 1978.

Malone, Dumas, *Jefferson And His Time*, 1981.

Padover, Saul K., *Jefferson*, 1942.

Randall, Willard, *Thomas Jefferson: A Life*, 1993.

Joseph, Chief of the Nez Perce
I Will Fight No More Forever
October 5, 1877

I said in my heart that I would give up my land. I would give up my father's grave. I would give up everything rather than have the blood of my people on my hands.   **- Chief Joseph (1877)**

The Nee-Me-Poo People, named by Lewis and Clark *The Nez Perce*, or Pierced-Nose Indians, were the largest native American tribe in the Pacific Northwest. The Northern tribes, the Upper Nez Perce, signed a Peace Treaty with the United States and agreed to move to an Indian reservation. The Southern tribes, the Lower Nez Perce, refused to sign what they called *The Theft Treaty*. One of the Lower Nez Perce tribes, living in the Wallowah (Winding Water) Valley of Oregon, was ruled by Thunder In The Mountains, named by Christian missionaries *Chief Joseph*.

The United States Government, claiming that their peace treaty was with all the Nez Perce tribes, ordered Chief Joseph to move his people onto the reservation. Joseph responded, *Some of the Nez Perce gave up their land. We never did. The earth is part of our body and we will never give up the earth.*

On June 15, 1877, the 1st U.S. Cavalry (5000 soldiers) was sent to move the Nez Perce onto the reservation. Chief Joseph's Nez Perce (300 warriors and 500 women and children) began a 1,200 mile retreat through Oregon, Idaho, Montana, and Wyoming to a hoped-for sanctuary in Canada. With the U.S. Cavalry in pursuit, between June 17 and October 5, Chief Joseph, who had never before led an army, fought eight battles against four separate forces.

On October 5, 1877, Chief Joseph, just thirty miles short of the Canadian border, was forced to surrender his Nez Perce tribe to the U.S. Army. At the surrender ceremony he made this landmark speech, *I Will Fight No More Forever.*

Chief Joseph

I am tired of fighting. Our chiefs are killed. Looking Glass is dead. Toohulhulsote is dead. The old men are all dead. It is the young men who say no and yes. He who led the young men is dead.

It is cold and we have no blankets. The little children are freezing to death. My people, some of them, have run away to the hills. And have no blankets, no food. No one knows where they are. Perhaps they are freezing to death. I want to have time to look for my children. And see how many of them I can find. Maybe I shall find them among the dead.

Hear me, my chiefs, I am tired. My heart is sad and sick. From where the sun now stands, I will fight no more forever.

Afterward

Chief Joseph was imprisoned first at Fort Lincoln, North Dakota, and then at Fort Leavenworth, Kansas. He was forced to live out his life on Oklahoma's Quapaw and Ponca Reservations, and finally Washington State's Colville Reservation, where he died on September 21, 1904.

Selected Reading

Beal, Merrill D., *"I Will Fight No More Forever": Chief Joseph and the Nez Perce War*, 1963.

Chalmers, Harvey, *The Last Stand of the Nez Perce: Destruction of a People*, 1962.

Davis, Russell G., and Brent Ashabranner, *Chief Joseph, War Chief of the Nez Perce*, 1962.

Hampton, Bruce, *Children of Grace: The Nez Perce War of 1877*, 1994.

Howard, Helen A., *Saga of Chief Joseph*, 1978.

Joseph, Nez Perce Chief, *Chief Joseph's Own Story*, 1983.

Robert E. Lee
Farewell To The Confederate Army
April 10, 1865

General Grant, I reciprocate your desire to avoid useless spilling of blood, and therefore ask the terms you will offer on surrender.
- General Robert E. Lee, April 8, 1865

On April 9, 1865, at Appomattox Courthouse, Virginia, Confederate General Robert E. Lee surrendered the Army of Northern Virginia to Federal General Ulysses S. Grant, effectively ending the American Civil War.

Robert Edward Lee was born on January 19, 1807 at Stratford Plantation, in Westmoreland County, Virginia, the son of Revolutionary War General Henry *Light Horse Harry* and Ann (Carter) Lee. Educated at the U.S. Military Academy at West Point, Lee served with distinction in the 1848 Mexican War. He commanded the forces that, on October 18, 1859, captured John Brown at Harper's Ferry, and he was Superintendent of West Point from 1852 to 1855. When, on April 20, 1861, Virginia seceded from the Union, Lee resigned from the U.S. Army. Confederate President Jefferson Davis appointed him to command the Army of Northern Virginia on May 31, 1862. The Army of Northern Virginia, under Lee's command, fought at the following battles - The Seven Days, Second Manassas/Second Bull Run, Sharpsburg/Antietam, Fredericksburg, Chancellorsville, Gettysburg, The Wilderness, Spotsylvania Courthouse, Cold Harbor, Petersburg, Five Forks, and Appomattox.

After surrendering the Army of Northern Virginia, General Robert E. Lee issued, on April 10, 1865, this landmark farewell address to his soldiers.

After four years of arduous service, marked by unsurpassed courage and fortitude, the Army of Northern Virginia has been compelled to yield to overwhelming numbers and resources. I need not tell the survivors of so many hard-fought battles, who have remained steadfast to the last, that I have consented to this result from no distrust of them, but, feeling that valor and devotion could accomplish nothing that could compensate for the loss that would have attended the continuation of the contest, I have determined to avoid the useless sacrifice of those whose past services have endeared them to their countrymen. By the terms of the agreement, officers and men can return to their homes and remain there until exchanged. You will take with you the satisfaction that proceeds from the consciousness of duty faithfully performed; and I earnestly pray that a merciful God will extend to you His blessing and protection. With an increasing admiration of your constancy and devotion to your country, and a grateful remembrance of your kind and generous consideration of myself, I bid you an affectionate farewell.

Robert E. Lee

Afterward

On April 12, 1865, Robert E. Lee explained his surrender to Confederate President Jefferson Davis, *The enemy was more than five times our number. If we could have forced our way one day longer, it would have been at a great sacrifice of life; at its end, I did not see how a surrender could have been avoided.* Robert E. Lee died on October 12, 1870.

Selected Reading

Bishop, Merrill, *The Gentleman Commander*, 1937.

Bradford, Gamaliel, Jr., *Lee the American*, 1940.

Bruce, Philip A., *Robert E. Lee*, 1907.

Dowdey, Clifford, *Lee*, 1965.

Freeman, Douglas, *R.E. Lee: A Biography*, 1935.

Maurice, Sir Frederick, *Robert E. Lee, The Soldier*, 1972.

Sanborn, Margaret, *Robert E. Lee*, 1966.

Thomas, Emory, *Robert E. Lee*, 1995.

White, Henry A., *Robert E. Lee*, 1969.

Abraham Lincoln

Abraham Lincoln was born on February 12, 1809 in Hardin County, Kentucky, the son of Thomas and Nancy (Hanks) Lincoln. Abraham Lincoln made two great speeches in his quest for the Presidency - 1858's House Divided Speech - *"A house divided against itself cannot stand." I believe this government cannot endure half slave and half free. I do not expect the Union to be dissolved - I do not expect the house to fall - but I do expect that it will cease to be divided.* - and 1860's Cooper Union Speech - *Let us have faith that might makes right, and in that faith, let us, to the end, dare to do our duty as we understand it.* Lincoln was elected President on November 6, 1860. The Civil War began on April 12, 1861. Lincoln's Emancipation Proclamation was issued on January 1, 1863 - *I, Abraham Lincoln, President of the United States, by virtue of the power invested in me, do declare that all persons held as slaves are, and henceforth shall be, forever free.* Lincoln went on to make two landmark speeches.

The Gettysburg Address
November 19, 1863

At the Battle of Gettysburg, July 1-3, 1863, the Union and Confederate Armies suffered an estimated 10,500 dead. On November 19, 1863, President Lincoln, invited to say *a few appropriate words* at the dedication ceremony of the Gettysburg National Cemetery, spoke for only three minutes, delivering his landmark *Gettysburg Address.*

The Second Inaugural Address
March 4, 1865

On November 8, 1864, President Abraham Lincoln was re-elected. The Civil War, which had cost the nation over 750,000 casualties, was ending. On March 4, 1865, to begin the national healing process, Lincoln, after taking the Presidential Oath of Office, delivered his landmark *Second Inaugural Address.*

Abraham Lincoln

The Gettysburg Address

Fourscore and seven years ago, our fathers brought forth on this continent a new nation, conceived in liberty, and dedicated to the proposition that all men are created equal.

Now we are engaged in a great civil war, testing whether that nation, or any nation so conceived and so dedicated, can long endure. We are met on a great battlefield of that war. We have come to dedicate a portion of that field as a final resting place for those who here gave their lives that that nation might live. It is altogether fitting and proper that we should do this.

But, in a larger sense, we cannot dedicate - we cannot consecrate - we cannot hallow - this ground. The brave men, living and dead, who struggled here, have consecrated it far above our poor power to add or detract. The world will little note nor long remember what we say here, but it can never forget what they did here.

It is for us, the living, rather, to be dedicated here to the unfinished work which they who fought here have thus far so nobly advanced. It is rather for us to be here dedicated to the great task remaining before us - that from these honored dead we take increased devotion to that cause for which they gave the last full measure of devotion - that we here highly resolve that these dead shall not have died in vain - that this nation, under God, shall have a new birth of freedom - and that government of the people, by the people, for the people, shall not perish from the earth.

Abraham Lincoln

The Second Inaugural Address

At this second appearing to take the oath of the Presidential office, there is less occasion for an extended address than there was at the first. Then a statement, somewhat in detail, of a course to be pursued, seemed fitting and proper. Now, at the expiration of four years, during which public declarations have been constantly called forth on every point and phase of the great contest which still absorbs the attention, and engrosses the energies of the nation, little that is new could be presented. The progress of our arms, upon which all else chiefly depends, is as well known to the public as to myself; and it is, I trust, reasonably satisfactory and encouraging to all. With high hope for the future, no prediction in regard to it is ventured.

On the occasion corresponding to this four years ago, all thoughts were anxiously directed to an impending civil war. All dreaded it - all sought to avert it. While the inaugural address was being delivered from this place, devoted altogether to *saving* the Union without war, insurgent agents were in the city seeking to *destroy* it without war - seeking to dissolve the Union, and divide effects, by negotiation. Both parties deprecated war; but one of them would *make* war rather than let the nation survive; and the other would *accept* war rather than let it perish. And the war came.

One eighth of the whole population were colored slaves, not distributed generally over the Union, but localized in the Southern part of it. These slaves constituted a peculiar and powerful interest. All knew that this interest was, somehow, the cause of the war. To strengthen, perpetuate, and extend this interest was the object for which the insurgents would rend the Union, even by war, while the government claimed no right to do more than to restrict the territorial enlargement of it. Neither party expected for the war, the magnitude, or the duration, which it has already attained. Neither anticipated that the *cause* of the conflict might cease with, or even before, the conflict itself should cease. Each looked for an easier triumph, and a result less fundamental and astounding. Both read the same bible, and pray to the same God; and each invokes His aid against the other. It may seem strange that any men should dare to ask a just God's assistance in wringing their bread from the sweat of other men's faces; but let us judge not that we be not judged. The prayers of both could not be answered; that of neither has been answered fully. The Almighty has his own purposes. *Woe unto the world because of offenses! for it must needs be that offenses come; but woe to that man by whom the offense cometh!* If we shall suppose that American slavery is one of those offenses which, in the providence of God, must needs come, but which, having continued through His appointed time, He now wills to remove, and that He gives to both North and South, this terrible war, as the woe due to those by whom the offense came, shall we discern therein any departure from those divine attributes which the believers in a Living God always ascribe to Him? Fondly do we hope - fervently do we pray - that this mighty scourge of war may speedily pass away. Yet, if God wills that it continue, until all the wealth piled by the bond-man's two hundred and fifty years of unrequited toil shall be sunk, and until every drop of blood drawn with the lash shall be paid by another drawn with the sword, as was said three thousand years ago, so still it must be said, *the judgments of the Lord, are true and righteous altogether.*

With malice toward none, with charity for all, with firmness in the right, as God gives us to see the right - let us strive on to finish the work we are in - to bind up the nation's wounds, to care for him who shall have borne the battle, and for his widow, and his orphan - to do all which may achieve and cherish a just and lasting peace, among our-selves, and with all nations.

Abraham Lincoln

Afterward

On the night of April 14, 1863, in Washington, D.C.'s Ford's Theater, John Wilkes Booth shot President Abraham Lincoln, who died on April 15, 1863.

Selected Reading

Harrison, Maureen, and Steve Gilbert, Editors, *Abraham Lincoln: Word for Word*, 1993.

Heidorf, Christian J., *Gettysburg: The One Hundred Twenty-Fifth Anniversary: What They Did Here*, 1990.

Lee, Andrew, *Lincoln*, 1989.

Randall, J.G., and Richard N. Current, *Lincoln the President: Last Full Measure*, 1991.

Sandburg, Carl, *Abraham Lincoln*, 1939.

Thomas, John L., *Abraham Lincoln and the American Political Tradition*, 1986.

Wills, Garry, *Lincoln at Gettysburg: The Words that Remade America, 1993*.

Luther Martin
The Treason Trial Of Aaron Burr
June 9, 1807

Luther Martin is an unprincipled and impudent bulldog.
- President Thomas Jefferson (1807)

The 1806 *Burr Conspiracy* was an alleged scheme formed by ex-Vice President Aaron Burr and General James Wilkinson to raise a Revolutionary Army and use it as a base to either take Mexico from Spain or the Western States from the United States. Wilkinson, fearful of exposure, wrote a letter to President Jefferson, pleading his own innocence and purportedly outlining Burr's *deep, dark, wicked, conspiracy.* Jefferson ordered the arrest of Burr on the charge of treason, stating publicly, *Of his guilt there can be no doubt.* A conviction for treason, the only crime defined by the Constitution, carried the death penalty. On May 22, 1807, in Richmond, Virginia, with Chief Justice John Marshall presiding, the treason trial of Aaron Burr began. Counsel for the defense was the *unprincipled and impudent bulldog,* Luther Martin.

Luther Martin was born in February 1748 near New Brunswick, New Jersey, the son of Benjamin and Hannah (Lennox) Martin. Educated at the College of New Jersey, Martin was admitted to the Maryland Bar in 1771 and rose to become Maryland's Attorney General. As a delegate to the 1791 Federal Constitutional Convention, he supported States' Rights and a separate Bill of Rights. Martin gained national fame (and earned President Jefferson's wrath) as defense counsel at the 1805 impeachment trial of Supreme Court Justice Samuel Chase.

On June 9, 1807, at the treason trial of Aaron Burr, Luther Martin made this landmark speech, demanding that President Jefferson be ordered to personally appear in Court with the supposedly incriminating Wilkinson Letter.

The question is whether the President can be summoned to attend with certain papers. One of them we want is an original letter from General Wilkinson, of the 21st of October, and received by the President on the 27th of November. This letter, as appears by Colonel Burr's affidavit, is considered by him as necessary to his defense, and his counsel, so far as they understand the subject, are of the same opinion. The other papers are copies of official orders by the Navy and War Departments. It may be said, sir, that if application were made to those Departments, Colonel Burr had a right to the papers, for we had supposed that every citizen was entitled to such copies of official papers as are material to him. And I have never heard of but one instance where they were refused, and this was most certainly under Presidential influence.

I have asserted that Colonel Burr was entitled to a copy of these orders. We intended to show that these orders were contrary to the Constitution and the laws, and that they entitled Colonel Burr to the right of resistance. We intended to show that by this particular order his property and his person were to be destroyed; yes, by these tyrannical orders the life and property of an innocent man were to be exposed to destruction. We did not expect these originals themselves. But we did apply for copies, and were refused under Presidential influence. In New York, on the farcical trials of Ogden and Smith, the officers of the government screened themselves from attending, under the sanction of the President's name. Perhaps the same farce may be repeated here, and it is for this reason that we apply directly to the President of the United States. Whether it would have been best to have applied to the Secretaries of State, of the Navy and War, I cannot say. All that we want is the copies of some papers, and the original of another. This is a peculiar case, sir. The President has undertaken to prejudge my client by declaring that, *Of his guilt there can be no doubt.* He has assumed to himself the knowledge of the Supreme Being himself, and pretended to search the heart of my highly respected friend. He has proclaimed him a traitor in the face of that country which has rewarded him. He has let slip the dogs of war, the hell-hounds of persecution, to hunt down my friend. And would this President of the United States, who has raised all this absurd clamor, pretend to keep back the papers which are wanted for this trial, where life itself is at stake? It is a sacred principle that in all such cases, the accused has a right to all the evidence which is necessary for his defense. And whoever withholds, willfully, information that would save the life of a person charged with a capital offense is substantially a murderer, and so recorded in the register of Heaven. Can it then be presumed that the President would be sorry to have Colonel Burr's innocence proved? No, it is impossible. Would the President of the United States give his enemies - for enemies he has, like other great and good men - would he give them the proud opportunity of saying that Colonel Burr is the victim of anger, jealousy, and hatred? Will he not act with all possible candor? When told that certain papers are material to our defense, will he not be proud to say to us, *Sirs, you may have them; I will grant you every possible advantage.* Had this been done, the attorney for the United States (and perhaps the Executive) never would have said that these papers are no more material to us than the first paragraph of the laws of Congress. These gentlemen forget that it is not their province to decide whether the evidence is material to us or not. It is for the court to say whether it bears upon the case, and whether it is to go before the petit jury, or to come before themselves, if the motion to commit for treason be continued.

They seem to think that we are not even to be trusted with these papers. But why do they attribute motives to Colonel

Burr's counsel, which they would themselves disdain? Why not do as much honor to ourselves as to the President of the United States himself?

It may be suggested that this is a private and confidential letter from General Wilkinson to the President. It was so said, indeed, yesterday. But if the President were here himself, the court would have a right to demand whether in confidential conversations General Wilkinson had not given very different statements from those which he might here produce? What, sir, if General Wilkinson had reposed as much confidence, if he had instilled as much poison into the ear of the President as Satan himself breathed into the ear of Eve? The President would have been still responsible to a court of justice, and bound to disclose his communications. The law recognizes none of this kind of confidence. I refer your honors to . . . [the case of the Duchess of Kingston]. There a physician entreated of the court to excuse him; but even his professional confidence (though of the most delicate nature) would not screen him. Lord Barrington in that case conjured them to excuse his giving in testimony what had been disclosed to him in all the confidence of private friendship. All his solicitations were disregarded. . . . Now let us suppose that this information was conveyed to him by a letter - nay, by a private and confidential letter - could we not have the President produced here; could we not examine him, whether he had ever received such a letter?

But perhaps we shall be told that this would be making too free with high characters, that we call the honor of General Wilkinson into question, and that it is not less than treason to suppose it possible that General Wilkinson is not as pure as an angel. But, sir, will it be forgotten that this man has already broken the Constitution to support his violent measures, that he has already ground down the civil authorities into dust, and subjected all around him to a military despotism? Is it possible to believe that such a man may not swerve from the strict line of rectitude and decorum? . . . [O]ne man may be destroyed by another man or by a faction, and with the same unfeeling indifference as a philosopher sees rats struggling in an air pump. . . .

Respecting copies of the Navy orders for destroying the property and person of Colonel Burr, it is very material to possess them. It may be necessary to show that these acts, which the prosecutors are pleased to deem treasonable, were in fact nothing but justifiable means for defending his own rights.

Afterward

Chief Justice Marshall ruled that, while President Jefferson would have to surrender the Wilkinson Letter, he would not have to surrender it in person. On August 31, 1807, after Luther Martin convinced a jury that the Wilkinson Letter contained no proof of his client's guilt, Aaron Burr was acquitted of the charge of treason. Martin was reappointed Maryland's Attorney General and in that capacity argued Maryland's cause in the landmark Supreme Court case, *McCulloch v. Maryland.*

Luther Martin died on July 8, 1826.

Selected Reading

Abernethy, Thomas, *The Burr Conspiracy,* 1968.
Beirne, Francis, *Shout Treason: The Trial of Aaron Burr,* 1959.
Brady, Joseph P., *The Trial of Aaron Burr,* 1913.
Chidsey, Donald, *The Great Conspiracy,* 1967.
Clarkson, Paul S., and R. Samuel Jett, *Luther Martin of Maryland,* 1970.
Martin, Luther, *Autobiography,* 1802.

James Monroe
The Monroe Doctrine
December 2, 1823

The American continent is henceforth not to be considered subject to future colonization by any European powers.
- President James Monroe, December 2, 1823

James Monroe was born on April 28, 1758 in Westmoreland County, Virginia, the son of Spense and Elizabeth (Jones) Monroe. After two years at the College of William and Mary, Monroe joined the Revolutionary Army. He studied law with Thomas Jefferson. Monroe served in the Continental Congress and in the U.S. Senate. He served as Governor of Virginia, and as President Jefferson's Minister to France, Spain, and England. On May 2, 1803, Monroe negotiated the Louisiana Purchase, which gave the United States enough land for thirteen new states. He served as President Madison's Secretary of State and negotiated the Treaty of Ghent, ending the War of 1812. On February 12, 1817, James Monroe was elected the fifth President of the United States.

The Spanish Empire in the Americas began to crumble and fall during the Monroe Presidency. On May 24, 1818, Monroe sent General Andrew Jackson to seize Spanish Florida. Monroe then recognized the independence from Spain of Mexico, Columbia, Venezuela, Ecuador, and Panama, and Chile, Peru, and Argentina. The Spanish Government began to prepare for a war to recover her former American colonies.

On December 2, 1823, as part of the State of the Union Address, President James Monroe set down his landmark *Keep your hands off the Americas* statement, *The Monroe Doctrine.*

James Monroe

Fellow citizens of the Senate and House of Representatives, many important subjects will claim your attention during the present session, of which I shall endeavor to give, in aid of your deliberations, a just idea in this communication. I undertake this duty with diffidence, from the vast extent of the interests on which I have to treat and of their great importance to every portion of our Union. I enter on it with zeal from a thorough conviction that there never was a period since the establishment of our Revolution when, regarding the condition of the civilized world and its bearing on us, there was greater necessity for devotion in the public servants to their respective duties, or for virtue, patriotism, and union in our constituents.

Meeting in you a new Congress, I deem it proper to present this view of public affairs in greater detail than might otherwise be necessary. I do it, however, with peculiar satisfaction, from a knowledge that in this respect I shall comply more fully with the sound principles of our Government. The people being with us exclusively the sovereign, it is indispensable that full information be laid before them on all important subjects, to enable them to exercise that high power with complete effect. If kept in the dark, they must be incompetent to it. We are all liable to error, and those who are engaged in the management of public affairs are more subject to excitement and to be led astray by their particular interests and passions than the great body of our constituents, who, living at home in the pursuit of their ordinary avocations, are calm but deeply interested spectators of events and of the conduct of those who are parties to them. To the people every department of the Government and every individual in each are responsible, and the more full their information the better they can judge of the wisdom of the policy pursued and of the conduct of each in regard to it. From their dispassionate judgment much aid may always be obtained, while their approbation will form the greatest incentive and most gratifying reward for virtuous actions, and the dread of their censure the best security against the abuse of their confidence. Their interests in all vital questions are the same, and the bond, by sentiment as well as by interest, will be proportionably strengthened as they are better informed of the real state of public affairs, especially in difficult conjunctures. It is by such knowledge that local prejudices and jealousies are surmounted, and that a national policy, extending its fostering care and protection to all the great interests of our Union, is formed and steadily adhered to.

A precise knowledge of our relations with foreign powers as respects our negotiations and transactions with each is thought to be particularly necessary. Equally necessary is it that we should form a just estimate of our resources, revenue, and progress in every kind of improvement connected with the national prosperity and public defense. It is by rendering justice to other nations that we may expect it from them. It is by our ability to resent injuries and redress wrongs that we may avoid them.

The commissioners under the fifth article of the Treaty of Ghent, having disagreed in their opinions respecting that portion of the boundary between the Territories of the United States and of Great Britain, the establishment of which had been submitted to them, have made their respective reports in compliance with that article, that the same might be referred to the decision of a friendly power. It being manifest, however, that it would be difficult, if not impossible, for any power to perform that office without great delay and much inconvenience to itself, a proposal has been made by this Government, and acceded to by that of

Great Britain, to endeavor to establish that boundary by amicable negotiation. It appearing from long experience that no satisfactory arrangement could be formed of the commercial intercourse between the United States and the British colonies in this hemisphere by legislative acts while each party pursued its own course without agreement or concert with the other, a proposal has been made to the British Government to regulate this commerce by treaty, as it has been to arrange in like manner the just claim of the citizens of the United States inhabiting the States and Territories bordering on the lakes and rivers which empty into the St. Lawrence to the navigation of that river to the ocean. For these and other objects of high importance to the interests of both parties, a negotiation has been opened with the British Government which it is hoped will have a satisfactory result.

The commissioners under the sixth and seventh articles of the Treaty of Ghent having successfully closed their labors in relation to the sixth, have proceeded to the discharge of those relating to the seventh. Their progress in the extensive survey required for the performance of their duties justifies the presumption that it will be completed in the ensuing year.

The negotiations which had been long depending with the French Government on several important subjects, and particularly for a just indemnity for losses sustained in the late wars by the citizens of the United States under unjustifiable seizures and confiscations of their property, has not as yet had the desired effect. As this claim rests on the same principle with others which have been admitted by the French Government, it is not perceived on what just ground it can be rejected. A minister will be immediately appointed to proceed to France and resume the negotiation on this and other subjects which may arise between the two nations.

At the proposal of the Russian Imperial Government, made through the minister of the Emperor residing here, a full power and instructions have been transmitted to the minister of the United States at St. Petersburg to arrange by amicable negotiation the respective rights and interests of the two nations on the northwest coast of this continent. A similar proposal had been made by His Imperial Majesty to the Government of Great Britain, which has likewise been acceded to. The Government of the United States has been desirous by this friendly proceeding of manifesting the great value which they have invariably attached to the friendship of the Emperor and their solicitude to cultivate the best understanding with his Government. In the discussions to which this interest has given rise and in the arrangements by which they may terminate, the occasion has been judged proper for asserting, as a principle in which the rights and interests of the United States are involved, that the American continents, by the free and independent condition which they have assumed and maintain, are henceforth not to be considered as subjects for future colonization by any European powers.

Since the close of the last session of Congress, the commissioners and arbitrators for ascertaining and determining the amount of indemnification which may be due to citizens of the United States under the decision of His Imperial Majesty, the Emperor of Russia, in conformity to the convention concluded at St. Petersburg on the 12th of July, 1822, have assembled in this city, and organized themselves as a board for the performance of the duties assigned to them by that treaty. The commission constituted under the eleventh article of the treaty of the 22d of February, 1819, between the United States and Spain, is also in session here, and as the term of three years limited by the treaty for the execution of the trust will expire before the period of the next regular meeting of Congress, the attention of the Legislature will be drawn to the measures which may be necessary to accomplish the objects for which the commission was instituted.

In compliance with a resolution of the House of Representatives adopted at their last session, instructions have been given to all the ministers of the United States accredited to the powers of Europe and America to propose the proscription of the African slave trade by classing it under the denomination, and inflicting on its perpetrators the punishment, of piracy. Should this proposal be acceded to, it is not doubted that this odious and criminal practice will be promptly and entirely suppressed. It is earnestly hoped that it will be acceded to, from the firm belief that it is the most effectual expedient that can be adopted for the purpose.

At the commencement of the recent war between France and Spain it was declared by the French Government that it would grant no commissions to privateers, and that neither the commerce of Spain herself nor of neutral nations should be molested by the naval force of France, except in the breach of a lawful blockade. This declaration, which appears to have been faithfully carried into effect, concurring with principles proclaimed and cherished by the United States from the first establishment of their independence, suggested the hope that the time had arrived when the proposal for adopting it as a permanent and invariable rule in all future maritime wars might meet the favorable consideration of the great European powers. Instructions have accordingly been given to our ministers with France, Russia, and Great Britain to make those proposals to their respective governments, and when the friends of humanity reflect on the essential amelioration to the condition of the human race which would result from the abolition of private war on the sea and on the great facility by which it might be accomplished, requiring only the consent of a few sovereigns, an earnest hope is indulged that these overtures will meet with an attention animated by the spirit in which they were made, and that they will ultimately be successful.

The ministers who were appointed to the Republics of Colombia and Buenos Aires during the last session of Congress proceeded shortly afterwards to their destinations. Of their arrival there official intelligence has not yet been received. The minister appointed to the Republic of Chile will sail in a few days. An early appointment will also be made to Mexico. A minister has been received from Colombia, and the other governments have been informed that ministers, or diplomatic agents of inferior grade, would be received from each, accordingly as they might prefer the one or the other.

The minister appointed to Spain proceeded soon after his appointment for Cadiz, the residence of the Sovereign to whom he was accredited. In approaching that port, the frigate which conveyed him was warned off by the commander of the French squadron by which it was blockaded and not permitted to enter, although apprised by the captain of the frigate of the public character of the person whom he had on board, the landing of whom was the sole object of his proposed entry. This act, being considered an infringement of the rights of ambassadors and of nations, will form a just cause of complaint to the Government of France against the officer by whom it was committed. . . .

A strong hope has been long entertained, founded on the heroic struggle of the Greeks, that they would succeed in their contest and resume their equal station among the nations of the earth. It is believed that the whole civilized world take a deep interest in their welfare. Although no power has declared in their favor, yet none, according to our information, has taken part against them. Their cause and their name have protected them from dangers which might ere this have overwhelmed any other people. The ordinary calculations of interest and of acquisition with a view to aggrandizement, which mingles so much in the transactions of nations, seems to have had no effect in regard to them. From the facts which have come to our knowledge there is good cause to believe that their enemy has lost forever all dominion over them, that Greece will become again an independent nation. That she may obtain that rank is the object of our most ardent wishes.

It was stated at the commencement of the last session that a great effort was then making in Spain and Portugal to improve the condition of the people of those countries, and that it appeared to be conducted with extraordinary moderation. It need scarcely be remarked that the result has been so far very different from what was then anticipated. Of events in that quarter of the globe, with which we have so much intercourse and from which we derive our origin, we have always been anxious and interested spectators. The citizens of the United States cherish sentiments the most friendly in favor of the liberty and happiness of their fellow men on that side of the Atlantic. In the wars of the European powers in matters relating to themselves we have never taken any part, nor does it comport with our policy to do so. It is only when our rights are invaded or seriously menaced that we resent injuries or make preparation for our defense. With the movements in this hemisphere we are of necessity more immediately connected, and by causes which must be obvious to all enlightened and impartial observers. The political system of the allied powers is essentially different in this respect from that of America. This difference proceeds from that which exists in their respective governments, and to the defense of our own, which has been achieved by the loss of so much blood and treasure, and matured by the wisdom of their most enlightened citizens, and under which we have enjoyed unexampled felicity, this whole nation is devoted. We owe it, therefore, to candor and to the amicable relations existing between the United States and those powers to declare that we should consider any attempt on their part to extend their system to any portion of this hemisphere as dangerous to our peace and safety. With the existing colonies or dependencies of any European power we have not interfered and shall not interfere. But with the governments who have declared their independence and maintained it, and whose independence we have, on great consideration and on just principles, acknowledged, we could not view any interposition for the purpose of oppressing them, or controlling in any other manner their destiny, by any European power in any other light than as the manifestation of an unfriendly disposition toward the United States. In the war between those new governments and Spain we declared our neutrality at the time of their recognition, and to this we have adhered, and shall continue to adhere, provided no change shall occur which, in the judgment of the competent authorities of this government, shall make a corresponding change on the part of the United States indispensable to their security.

The late events in Spain and Portugal show that Europe is still unsettled. Of this important fact no stronger proof can be adduced than that the allied powers should have thought it proper, on any principle satisfactory to themselves, to have interposed by force in the internal concerns of Spain. To what extent such interposition may be carried, on the same principle, is a question in which all independent powers whose governments differ from theirs are interested, even those most remote, and surely none more so than the United States. Our policy in regard to Europe, which was adopted at an early stage of the wars which have so long agitated that quarter of the globe, nevertheless remains the same, which is not to interfere in the internal concerns of any of its powers; to consider the government de facto as the legitimate government for us; to cultivate friendly relations with it, and to preserve those relations by a frank, firm, and manly policy, meeting in all instances the just claims of every power, submitting to injuries from none. But in regard to those continents circumstances are eminently and conspicuously different. It is impossible that the allied powers should extend their political system to any portion of either continent without endangering our peace and happiness; nor can anyone believe that our southern brethren, if left to themselves, would adopt it of their own accord. It is equally impossible, therefore, that we should behold such interposition in any form with indifference. If we look to the comparative strength and resources of Spain and those new Governments, and their distance from each other, it must be obvious that she can never subdue them. It is still the true policy of the United States to leave the parties to themselves, in the hope that other powers will pursue the same course.

If we compare the present condition of our Union with its actual state at the close of our Revolution, the history of the world furnishes no example of a progress in improvement in all the important circumstances which constitute the happiness of a nation which bears any resemblance to it. At the first epoch our population did not exceed

3,000,000. By the last census it amounted to about 10,000,000, and, what is more extraordinary, it is almost altogether native, for the immigration from other countries has been inconsiderable. At the first epoch half the territory within our acknowledged limits was uninhabited and a wilderness. Since then new territory has been acquired of vast extent, comprising within it many rivers, particularly the Mississippi, the navigation of which to the ocean was of the highest importance to the original States. Over this territory our population has expanded in every direction, and new States have been established almost equal in number to those which formed the first bond of our Union. This expansion of our population and accession of new States to our Union have had the happiest effect on all its highest interests. That it has eminently augmented our resources and added to our strength and respectability as a power is admitted by all. But it is not in these important circumstances only that this happy effect is felt. It is manifest that by enlarging the basis of our system and increasing the number of States the system itself has been greatly strengthened in both its branches. Consolidation and disunion have thereby been rendered equally impracticable. Each Government, confiding in its own strength, has less to apprehend from the other, and in consequence each, enjoying a greater freedom of action, is rendered more efficient for all the purposes for which it was instituted. It is unnecessary to treat here of the vast improvement made in the system itself by the adoption of this Constitution and of its happy effect in elevating the character and in protecting the rights of the nation as well as of individuals. To what, then, do we owe these blessings? It is known to all that we derive them from the excellence of our institutions. Ought we not, then, to adopt every measure which may be necessary to perpetuate them?

James Monroe

Afterward

The Monroe Doctrine effectively ended European interference in the Western Hemisphere. John Quincy Adams in his eulogy for James Monroe said, *He was entitled to say, like Augustus Caesar said of Rome, that he had found America built of brick and left her constructed of marble.*

James Monroe died on July 4, 1831.

Selected Reading

Ammon, Harry, *James Monroe: The Quest for National Identity*, 1971.

Brown, Stuart G., Editor, *The Autobiography of James Monroe*, 1959.

Cresson, W. P., *James Monroe*, 1971.

Cunningham, Noble E., Jr., *The Presidency of James Monroe*, 1996.

Gilman, Daniel C., *James Monroe*, 1911.

Morgan, George, *The Life of James Monroe*, 1969.

Styron, Arthur, *The Last of the Cocked Hats: James Monroe & the Virginia Dynasty*, 1945.

Gouverneur Morris
The Death Of Alexander Hamilton
July 14, 1804

*To those who, with me, abhorring the practice of dueling, may think
that I ought on no account to have added to the number of bad examples, I answer that my relative situation, as well in public as private
appeals, enforcing all the considerations which constitute what men of
the world denominate honor, impressed on me (as I thought) a peculiar
necessity not to decline the call. The ability to be in future useful,
whether in resisting mischief or effecting good, in those crises of our
public affairs, which seem likely to happen, would probably be inseparable from a conformity with public prejudice in this particular.*

- Alexander Hamilton, June 27, 1804

On the morning of July 11, 1804, in a duel over personal
insults between bitter political rivals, Aaron Burr mortally
wounded Alexander Hamilton. The death of Alexander
Hamilton, on July 12, 1804, at age forty-nine, sent the nation into mourning. Hamilton's oldest and closest friend,
Gouverneur Morris, was selected to deliver the eulogy.

Gouverneur Morris was born on January 30, 1752 on his
family's estate, Morrisania (now in the Bronx, New York),
the son of Lewis and Sarah (Gouverneur) Morris. After
graduating from King's College in 1768, Morris studied law
and entered politics. He served in the Continental Congress. In 1786, as a delegate to the Federal Constitutional
Convention, Morris is credited with drafting the Preamble
to the Constitution, *We, the people of the United States, in order
to form a more perfect union, establish justice, insure domestic tran-
quility, provide for the common defense, promote the general welfare,
and secure the blessings of liberty to ourselves and our posterity.*

On July 14, 1804, Gouverneur Morris delivered this landmark eulogy for Alexander Hamilton at New York City's
Trinity Church.

If on this sad, this solemn occasion, I should endeavor to move your commiseration, it would be doing injustice to that sensibility which has been so generally and so justly manifested. Far from attempting to excite your emotions, I must try to repress my own; and yet, I fear that, instead of the language of a public speaker, you will hear only the lamentations of a wailing friend. But I will struggle with my bursting heart to portray that heroic spirit which has flown to the mansions of bliss.

Students of Columbia - he was in the ardent pursuit of knowledge in your academic shades, when the first sound of the American war called him to the field. A young and un-protected volunteer, such was his zeal, and so brilliant his service, that we heard his name before we knew his person. It seemed as if God had called him suddenly into existence, that he might assist to save a world!

The penetrating eye of Washington soon perceived the manly spirit which animated his youthful bosom. By that excellent judge of men he was selected as an aide, and thus he became early acquainted with, and was a principal actor in, the more important scenes of our Revolution. At the siege of York, he pertinaciously insisted on, and he ob-tained the command of a Forlorn Hope. He stormed the redoubt; but let it be recorded that not one single man of the enemy perished. His gallant troops, emulating the hero-ism of their chief, checked the uplifted arm, and spared a foe no longer resisting. Here closed his military career.

Shortly after the war, your favor - no, your discernment, called him to public office. You sent him to the convention at Philadelphia; he here assisted in forming that Constitu-tion which is now the bond of our union, the shield of our defense, and the source of our prosperity. In signing the compact, he expressed his apprehension that it did not contain sufficient means of strength for its own preservation; and that in consequence we should share the fate of many other republics, and pass through anarchy to despotism. We hoped better things. We confided in the good sense of the American people; and, above all, we trusted in the protecting providence of the Almighty. On this important subject he never concealed his opinion. He disdained concealment. Knowing the purity of his heart, he bore it as it were in his hand, exposing to every passenger its inmost recesses. This generous indiscretion subjected him to censure from misrepresentation. His speculative opinions were treated as deliberate designs; and yet you all know how strenuous, how unremitting were his efforts to establish and to preserve the Constitution. If, then, his opinion was wrong, pardon, O! pardon that single error, in a life devoted to your service.

At the time when our government was organized, we were without funds, though not without resources. To call them into action, and establish order in the finances, Washington sought for splendid talents, for extensive information, and above all, he sought for sterling, incorruptible integrity. All these he found in Hamilton. The system then adopted has been the subject of much animadversion. If it be not without a fault, let it be remembered that nothing human is perfect. Recollect the circumstances of the moment - recollect the conflict of opinion - and, above all, remember that a minister of a republic must bend to the will of the people. The administration which Washington formed was one of the most efficient, one of the best that any country was ever blest with. And the result was a rapid advance in power and prosperity, of which there is no example in any other age or nation. The part which Hamilton bore is universally known.

His unsuspecting confidence in professions, which he believed to be sincere, led him to trust too much to the undeserving. This exposed him to misrepresentation. He felt himself obliged to resign. The care of a rising family, and the narrowness of his fortune, made it a duty to return to his profession for their support. But though he was compelled to abandon public life, never, no, never for a moment did he abandon the public service. He never lost sight of your interest. I declare to you before that God in whose presence we are now especially assembled that in his most private and confidential conversations, the single objects of discussion and consideration were your freedom and happiness. You well remember the state of things which again called forth Washington from his retreat to lead your armies. You know that he asked for Hamilton to be his second in command. That venerable sage well knew the dangerous incidents of a military profession, and he felt the hand of time pinching life at its source. It was probable that he would soon be removed from the scene, and that his second would succeed to the command. He knew by experience the importance of that place - and he thought the sword of America might safely be confided to the hand which now lies cold in that coffin. O! my fellow-citizens, remember this solemn testimonial that he was not ambitious. Yet he was charged with ambition, and wounded by the imputation; when he laid down his command, he declared, in the proud independence of his soul, that he never would accept of any office, unless in a foreign war he should be called on to expose his life in defense of his country. This determination was immovable. It was his fault that his opinions and his resolutions could not be changed.

Knowing his own firm purpose, he was indignant at the charge that he sought for place or power. He was ambitious only for glory, but he was deeply solicitous for you. For himself he feared nothing; but he feared that bad men might, by false professions, acquire your confidence, and abuse it to your ruin.

Brethren of the Cincinnati - there lies our chief! Let him still be our model. Like him, after long and faithful public services, let us cheerfully perform the social duties of private life. O! he was mild and gentle. In him there was no offense, no guile. His generous hand and heart were open to all. Gentlemen of the bar - you have lost your brightest ornament. Cherish and imitate his example. While, like him, with justifiable and with laudable zeal, you pursue the interests of your clients, remember, like him, the eternal principle of justice. Fellow-citizens - you have long witnessed his professional conduct, and felt his unrivaled eloquence. You know how well he performed the duties of a citizen - you know that he never courted your favor by adulation or the sacrifice of his own judgment. You have seen him contending against you, and saving your dearest interests, as it were, in spite of yourselves. And you now feel and enjoy the benefits resulting from the firm energy of his conduct. Bear this testimony to the memory of my departed friend. I charge you to protect his fame. It is all he has left - all that these poor orphan children will inherit from their father. But, my countrymen, that fame may be a rich treasure to you also. Let it be the test which to examine those who solicit your favor. Disregarding professions, view their conduct, and on a doubtful occasion ask, would Hamilton have done this thing? You all know how he perished. On this last scene I cannot, I must not dwell. It might excite emotions too strong for your better judgment. Suffer not your indignation to lead to any act which might again offend the in-sulted majesty of the laws. On his part, as from his lips, though with my voice - for his voice you will hear no more - let me entreat you to respect yourselves.

And now, ye ministers of the everlasting God, perform your holy office, and commit these ashes of our departed brother to the bosom of the grave.

Afterward
Gouverneur Morris died on November 6, 1816.

Selected Reading

Kline, Mary-Jo, *Gouverneur Morris and the New Nation, 1775-1788*, 1978.

Mintz, Max M., *Gouverneur Morris and the American Revolution*, 1970.

Morris, Anne Cary, Editor, *The Diary and Letters of Gouverneur Morris*, 1970.

Sparks, Jared, *The Life Of Gouverneur Morris*, 1832.

Syrett, H., Editor, *Interview In Weehawken*, 1960.

Theodore Roosevelt
The Strenuous Life
April 10, 1899

Any man who has ever been honored by being made President of the United States is thereby forever after rendered the debtor of the American people. **- Theodore Roosevelt (1910)**

Theodore Roosevelt, Jr., known to generations of Americans as *TR*, was born on October 27, 1858 in New York City, the child of Theodore, Sr. and Martha (Bulloch) Roosevelt. Educated at Harvard College - *The man with the university education is honor bound to take an active part in our political life.* - Roosevelt was a writer - *The Winning of the West, Good Hunting, The Strenuous Life* - and a conservationist - *It is not what we have that will make us a great nation; it is the way in which we use it.* He served as a New York legislator - *I would rather go out of politics feeling that I had done what was right than stay in politics knowing in my heart I had acted as I ought not to.* - as U.S. Civil Service Commissioner - *We can as little afford to tolerate a dishonest man in the public service as a coward in the army.* - and as Assistant Secretary of the Navy - *A nation should never fight unless forced to; but it should always be ready to fight.* As Colonel of the First United States Volunteer Cavalry Regiment, he led the *Rough Riders* in the July 1, 1899 charge up San Juan Hill - *We had a bully fight in Cuba. The charge was great fun.* He was Governor of New York from 1898 to 1900 - *The most successful politician is he who says what everyone is thinking most often and in the loudest voice.* - and Vice President of the United States from 1900 to 1901 - *I know how hollow the honor is.* He served as President of the United States from 1901 to 1909 - *The Presidency is a bully pulpit!*

On April 10, 1899, in Chicago, Illinois, while on a national speaking tour, Theodore Roosevelt delivered this landmark speech, *The Strenuous Life*.

In speaking to you men of the greatest city of the West, men of the State which gave to the country Lincoln and Grant, men who preeminently and distinctly embody all that is most American in the American character, I wish to preach, not the doctrine of ignoble ease, but the doctrine of the strenuous life, the life of toil and effort, of labor and strife - to preach that highest form of success which comes, not to the man who desires mere easy peace, but to the man who does not shrink from danger, from hardship, or from bitter toil, and who out of these wins the splendid ultimate triumph.

A life of slothful ease, a life of that peace which springs merely from lack either of desire or of power to strive after great things, is as little worthy of a nation as of an individual. I ask only that what every self-respecting American demands from himself and from his sons shall be demanded of the American nation as a whole. Who among you would teach your boys that ease, that peace, is to be the first consideration in their eyes - to be the ultimate goal after which they strive? You men of Chicago have made this city great; you men of Illinois have done your share, and more than your share, in making America great, because you neither preach nor practice such a doctrine. You work yourselves, and you bring up your sons to work. If you are rich and are worth your salt, you will teach your sons that though they may have leisure, it is not to be spent in idleness, for wisely used leisure merely means that those who possess it, being free from the necessity of working for their livelihood, are all the more bound to carry on some kind of non-remunerative work in science, in letters, in art, in exploration, in historical research - work of the type we most need in this country, the successful carrying out of which reflects most honor upon the nation. We do not ad-

mire the man of timid peace. We admire the man who em-
bodies victorious effort - the man who never wrongs his
neighbor, who is prompt to help a friend, but who has
those virile qualities necessary to win in the stern strife of
actual life. It is hard to fail, but it is worse never to have
tried to succeed. In this life we get nothing save by effort.
Freedom from effort in the present merely means that
there has been stored up effort in the past. A man can be
freed from the necessity of work only by the fact that he or
his fathers before him have worked to good purpose. If the
freedom thus purchased is used aright, and the man still
does actual work, though of a different kind, whether as a
writer or a general, whether in the field of politics or in the
field of exploration and adventure, he shows he deserves
his good fortune. But if he treats this period of freedom
from the need of actual labor as a period, not of preparation, but of mere enjoyment, even though perhaps not of
vicious enjoyment, he shows that he is simply a cumberer
of the earth's surface, and he surely unfits himself to hold
his own with his fellows if the need to do so should again
arise. A mere life of ease is not in the end a very satisfactory
life, and, above all, it is a life which ultimately unfits those
who follow it for serious work in the world.

In the last analysis a healthy state can exist only when the
men and women who make it up lead clean, vigorous,
healthy lives - when the children are so trained that they
shall endeavor, not to shirk difficulties, but to overcome
them - not to seek ease, but to know how to wrest triumph
from toil and risk. The man must be glad to do a man's
work, to dare and endure and to labor - to keep himself,
and to keep those dependent upon him. The woman must
be the housewife, the helpmeet of the homemaker, the
wise and fearless mother of many healthy children. In one
of Daudet's powerful and melancholy books he speaks of

the fear of maternity, the haunting terror of the young wife of the present day. When such words can be truthfully written of a nation, that nation is rotten to the heart's core. When men fear work or fear righteous war, when women fear motherhood, they tremble on the brink of doom - and well it is that they should vanish from the earth, where they are fit subjects for the scorn of all men and women who are themselves strong and brave and high-minded.

As it is with the individual, so it is with the nation. It is a base untruth to say that happy is the nation that has no history. Thrice happy is the nation that has a glorious history. Far better it is to dare mighty things, to win glorious triumphs, even though checkered by failure, than to take rank with those poor spirits who neither enjoy much nor suffer much, because they live in the gray twilight that knows not victory nor defeat. If in 1861 the men who loved the Union had believed that peace was the end of all things, and war and strife the worst of all things, and had acted up to their belief, we would have saved hundreds of thousands of lives - we would have saved hundreds of millions of dollars. Moreover, besides saving all the blood and treasure we then lavished, we would have prevented the heartbreak of many women, the dissolution of many homes, and we would have spared the country those months of gloom and shame when it seemed as if our armies marched only to defeat. We could have avoided all this suffering simply by shrinking from strife. And if we had thus avoided it, we would have shown that we were weaklings, and that we were unfit to stand among the great nations of the earth. Thank God for the iron in the blood of our fathers, the men who upheld the wisdom of Lincoln, and bore sword or rifle in the armies of Grant! Let us, the children of the men who proved themselves equal to the mighty days - let us, the children of the men who carried the great Civil War to a triumphant conclusion - praise the God of our fathers that the ignoble counsels of peace were rejected, that the suffering and loss, the blackness of sorrow and despair, were unflinchingly faced, and the years of strife endured - for in the end the slave was freed, the Union restored, and the mighty American republic placed once more as a helmeted queen among nations.

We of this generation do not have to face a task such as that our fathers faced, but we have our tasks, and woe to us if we fail to perform them! We cannot, if we would, play the part of China, and be content to rot by inches in ignoble ease within our borders, taking no interest in what goes on beyond them, sunk in a scrambling commercialism, heedless of the higher life, the life of aspiration, of toil and risk, busying ourselves only with the wants of our bodies for the day, until suddenly we should find, beyond a shadow of question, what China has already found - that in this world, the nation that has trained itself to a career of unwarlike and isolated ease is bound, in the end, to go down before other nations which have not lost the manly and adventurous qualities. If we are to be a really great people, we must strive in good faith to play a great part in the world. We cannot avoid meeting great issues. All that we can determine for ourselves is whether we shall meet them well or ill. In 1898 we could not help being brought face to face with the problem of war with Spain. All we could decide was whether we should shrink like cowards from the contest, or enter into it as beseemed a brave and high-spirited people, and, once in, whether failure or success should crown our banners. So it is now. We cannot avoid the responsibilities that confront us in Hawaii, Cuba, Puerto Rico, and the Philippines. All we can decide is whether we shall meet them in a way that will redound to the national credit, or whether we shall make of our dealings with these new problems a dark and shameful page in our history. To refuse to deal with them at all merely amounts to dealing with them badly. We have a given problem to solve. If we undertake the solution, there is, of course, always danger that we may not solve it aright; but to refuse to undertake the solution simply renders it certain that we cannot possibly solve it aright. The timid man, the lazy man, the man who distrusts his country, the over-civilized man, who has lost the great fighting, masterful virtues, the ignorant man, and the man of dull mind, whose soul is incapable of feeling the mighty lift that thrills *stern men with empires in their brains* - all these, of course, shrink from seeing the nation undertake its new duties, shrink from seeing us build a navy and an army adequate to our needs, shrink from seeing us do our share of the world's work, by bringing order out of chaos in the great, fair tropic islands from which the valor of our soldiers and sailors has driven the Spanish flag. These are the men who fear the strenuous life, who fear the only national life which is really worth leading. They believe in that cloistered life which saps the hardy virtues in a nation, as it saps them in the individual; or else they are wedded to that base spirit of gain and greed which recognizes in commercialism the be-all and end-all of national life, instead of realizing that, though an indispensable element, it is, after all, but one of the many elements that go to make up true national greatness. No country can long endure if its foundations are not laid deep in the material prosperity which comes from thrift, from business energy and enterprise, from hard, unsparing effort in the fields of industrial activity; but neither was any nation ever yet truly great if it relied upon material prosperity alone. All honor must be paid to the architects of our material prosperity, to the great captains of industry who have built our factories and our railroads, to the strong men who toil for wealth with brain or hand; for great is the debt of the nation to these and their kind. But our debt is yet greater to the men whose highest type is to be found in a statesman like Lincoln, a soldier like Grant. They showed by their lives that they recognized the law of work, the law of strife; they toiled to win a competence for themselves and those dependent upon them; but they recognized that there were yet other and even loftier duties - duties to the nation and duties to the race.

We cannot sit huddled within our own borders and avow ourselves merely an assemblage of well-to-do hucksters who care nothing for what happens beyond. Such a policy would defeat even its own end, for as the nations grow to have ever wider and wider interests, and are brought into closer and closer contact, if we are to hold our own in the struggle for naval and commercial supremacy, we must build up our power without our own borders. We must build the isthmian canal, and we must grasp the points of vantage which will enable us to have our say in deciding the destiny of the oceans of the East and the West.

So much for the commercial side. From the standpoint of international honor the argument is even stronger. The guns that thundered off Manila and Santiago left us echoes of glory, but they also left us a legacy of duty. If we drove out a medieval tyranny only to make room for savage anarchy, we had better not have begun the task at all. It is worse than idle to say that we have no duty to perform, and can leave to their fates the islands we have conquered. Such a course would be the course of infamy. It would be followed at once by utter chaos in the wretched islands themselves. Some stronger, manlier power would have to step in and do the work, and we would have shown ourselves weaklings, unable to carry to successful completion the labors that great and high-spirited nations are eager to undertake.

The work must be done; we cannot escape our responsibility; and if we are worth our salt, we shall be glad of the chance to do the work - glad of the chance to show ourselves equal to one of the great tasks set modern civilization. But let us not deceive ourselves as to the importance of the task. Let us not be misled by vainglory into underestimating the strain it will put on our powers. Above all, let us, as we value our own self-respect, face the responsibilities with proper seriousness, courage, and high resolve. We must demand the highest order of integrity and ability in our public men who are to grapple with these new problems. We must hold to a rigid accountability those public servants who show unfaithfulness to the interests of the nation or inability to rise to the high level of the new demands upon our strength and our resources.

Of course we must remember not to judge any public servant by any one act, and especially should we beware of attacking the men who are merely the occasions and not the causes of disaster. Let me illustrate what I mean by the Army and the Navy. If twenty years ago we had gone to war, we should have found the Navy as absolutely unprepared as the Army. At that time our ships could not have encountered with success the fleets of Spain any more than nowadays we can put untrained soldiers, no matter how brave, who are armed with archaic black-powder weapons, against well-drilled regulars armed with the highest-type of modern repeating rifle. But in the early eighties the attention of the nation became directed to our naval needs. Congress most wisely made a series of appropriations to build up a new Navy, and under a succession of able and patriotic Secretaries, of both political parties, the Navy was gradually built up, until its material became equal to its splendid personnel, with the result that in the summer of 1898 it leaped to its proper place as one of the most brilliant and formidable fighting navies in the entire world. We rightly pay all honor to the men controlling the Navy at the time it won these great deeds, honor to Secretary Long and Admiral Dewey, to the captains who handled the ships in action, to the daring lieutenants who braved death in the smaller craft, and to the heads of bureaus at Washington who saw that the ships were so commanded, so armed, so equipped, so well engined, as to insure the best results. But let us also keep ever in mind that all of this would not have availed if it had not been for the wisdom of the men who during the preceding fifteen years had built up the Navy. Keep in mind the Secretaries of the Navy during those years; keep in mind the Senators and Congressmen who by their votes gave the money necessary to build and to armor the ships, to construct the great guns, and to train the crews; remember also those who actually did build the ships, the armor, and the guns; and remember the admirals and the captains who handled battleship, cruiser, and torpedo boat on the high seas, alone and in squadrons, developing the seamanship, the gunnery, and the power of acting together, which their successors utilized so gloriously at Manila and off Santiago. And, gentlemen, remember the converse, too. Remember that justice has two sides. Be just to those who built up the Navy, and, for the sake of the future of the country, keep in mind those who opposed its building up. Read the Congressional Record. Find out the Senators and Congressmen who opposed the grants for building the new ships - who opposed the purchase of armor, without which the ships were worthless - who opposed any adequate maintenance for the Navy Department, and strove to cut down the number of men necessary to man our fleets. The men who did these things were one and all working to bring disaster on the country. They have no share in the glory of Manila, in the honor of Santiago. They have no cause to feel proud of the valor of our sea captains, of the renown of our flag. Their motives may or may not have been good, but their acts were heavily fraught with evil. They did ill for the national honor, and we won in spite of their sinister opposition.

Now, apply all this to our public men of today. Our Army has never been built up as it should be built up. I shall not discuss with an audience like this the puerile suggestion that a nation of seventy millions of freemen is in danger of losing its liberties from the existence of an army of one hundred thousand men, three-fourths of whom will be employed in certain foreign islands, in certain coast fortresses, and on Indian reservations. No man of good sense and stout heart can take such a proposition seriously. If we are such weaklings as the proposition implies, then we are unworthy of freedom in any event. To no body of men in the United States is the country so much indebted as to the splendid officers and enlisted men of the regular Army and Navy. There is no body from which the country has less to fear, and none of which it should be prouder, none which it should be more anxious to upbuild.

Our Army needs complete reorganization - not merely enlarging - and the reorganization can only come as the result of legislation. A proper general staff should be established, and the positions of ordnance, commissary, and quartermaster officers should be filled by detail from the line. Above all, the Army must be given the chance to exercise in large bodies. Never again should we see, as we saw in the Spanish war, major-generals in command of divisions who had never before commanded three companies together in the field. Yet, incredible to relate, Congress has shown a queer inability to learn some of the lessons of the war. There were large bodies of men in both branches who opposed the declaration of war, who opposed the ratification of peace, who opposed the upbuilding of the Army, and who even opposed the purchase of armor at a reasonable price for the battleships and cruisers, thereby putting an absolute stop to the building of any new fighting ships for the Navy. If, during the years to come, any disaster should befall our arms, afloat or ashore, and thereby any shame come to the United States, remember that the blame will lie upon the men whose names appear upon the roll calls of Congress on the wrong side of these great questions. On them will lie the burden of any loss of our soldiers and sailors, of any dishonor to the flag; and upon you and the people of this country will lie the blame if you do not repudiate, in no unmistakable way, what these men have done. The blame will not rest upon the untrained commander of untried troops, upon the civil officers of a department the organization of which has been left utterly inadequate, or upon the admiral with an insufficient number of ships - but upon the public men who have so lamentably failed in forethought as to refuse to remedy these evils long in advance, and upon the nation that stands behind those public men.

So, at the present hour, no small share of the responsibility for the blood shed in the Philippines, the blood of our brothers, and the blood of their wild and ignorant foes, lies at the thresholds of those who so long delayed the adoption of the treaty of peace, and of those who by their worse than foolish words deliberately invited a savage people to plunge into a war fraught with sure disaster for them - a war, too, in which our own brave men who follow the flag must pay with their blood for the silly, mock humanitarianism of the prattlers who sit at home in peace.

The Army and the Navy are the sword and the shield which this nation must carry if she is to do her duty among the nations of the earth - if she is not to stand merely as the China of the Western Hemisphere. Our proper conduct toward the tropic islands we have wrested from Spain is merely the form which our duty has taken at the moment. Of course we are bound to handle the affairs of our own household well. We must see that there is civic honesty, civic cleanliness, civic good sense in our home administration of city, state, and nation. We must strive for honesty in office, for honesty toward the creditors of the nation and of the individual, for the widest freedom of individual initiative where possible, and for the wisest control of individual initiative where it is hostile to the welfare of the many. But because we set our own household in order we are not thereby excused from playing our part in the great affairs of the world. A man's first duty is to his own home, but he is not thereby excused from doing his duty to the State, for if he fails in this second duty it is under the penalty of ceasing to be a freeman. In the same way, while a nation's first duty is within its own borders, it is not thereby absolved from facing its duties in the world as a whole; and if it refuses to do so, it merely forfeits its right to struggle for a place among the peoples that shape the destiny of mankind.

In the West Indies and the Philippines alike, we are confronted by most difficult problems. It is cowardly to shrink from solving them in the proper way, for solved they must be, if not by us, then by some stronger and more manful race. If we are too weak, too selfish, or too foolish to solve them, some bolder and abler people must undertake the solution. Personally, I am far too firm a believer in the greatness of my country and the power of my countrymen to admit for one moment that we shall ever be driven to the ignoble alternative.

. . . . I preach to you, then, my countrymen, that our country calls not for the life of ease but for the life of strenuous endeavor. The twentieth century looms before us big with the fate of many nations. If we stand idly by, if we seek merely swollen, slothful ease and ignoble peace, if we shrink from the hard contests where men must win at hazard of their lives and at the risk of all they hold dear, then the bolder and stronger peoples will pass us by, and will win for themselves the domination of the world. Let us therefore boldly face the life of strife - resolute to do our duty well and manfully - resolute to uphold righteousness by deed and by word - resolute to be both honest and brave, to serve high ideals, yet to use practical methods. Above all, let us shrink from no strife, moral or physical, within or without the nation, provided we are certain that the strife is justified, for it is only through strife, through hard and dangerous endeavor, that we shall ultimately win the goal of true national greatness.

Afterward
Theodore Roosevelt led the strenuous life until his death on January 6, 1919.

Selected Reading
Brands, H. W., *T. R.: The Last Romantic*, Basic Books, 1997.
Lorant, Stefan, *The Life and Times of Theodore Roosevelt*, 1959.
Morris, Edmund, *The Rise of Theodore Roosevelt*, 1979.
Naylor, Natalie A., Douglas Brinkley, and John Allen Gable, Editors, *Theodore Roosevelt, Many-Sided American*, 1992.
Wagenknecht, Edward, *The Seven Worlds of Theodore Roosevelt*, 1958.

William Seward
The Irrepressible Conflict
October 25, 1858

I know that I have spoken words that will tell when I am dead, and even while I am living, for the benefit and blessing of mankind, and for myself this is consolation enough.   **- William Seward**

William Henry Seward, one of the great anti-slavery speakers, was born on May 16, 1801 in Florida, New York, the child of Samuel and Mary (Jennings) Seward. William Seward attended Schenectady, New York's Union College and began to practice law in 1822. He served as a New York State Senator, as New York's Governor, and, in 1849, as a U.S. Senator.

In the pre-Civil War *shouting match* between Northern anti-slavery and Southern pro-slavery politicians, no one shouted louder than New York State's U.S. Senator William Henry Seward. On March 11, 1850, during the Senate's debate on Henry Clay's *Compromise of 1850*, Seward delivered a fervent anti-slavery speech, the *Higher Law* speech, which made him famous throughout the North and infamous throughout the South - *The Constitution regulates our stewardship. But there is a higher law than the Constitution which regulates our authority.* On February 17, 1854, during the Senate's debate on Stephen Douglas' *Kansas-Nebraska Act*, Seward delivered a second famous anti-slavery speech, *The Eternal Conflict* speech, which increased his position as the leading anti-slavery spokesman - *Senator Douglas' Kansas-Nebraska Bill illustrates the eternal conflict between conservatism and progress, between truth and error, between right and wrong.*

On October 25, 1858, in Rochester, New York, William Seward, while campaigning for the 1860 Republican Presidential nomination, delivered this landmark anti-slavery speech, *The Irrepressible Conflict.*

Our country is a theater which exhibits in full operation two radically different political systems - the one resting on the basis of servile or slave labor, the other on the basis of voluntary labor of freemen.

The laborers who are enslaved are all negroes, or persons more or less purely of African derivation. But this is only accidental. The principle of the system is that labor in every society, by whomsoever performed, is necessarily unintellectual, groveling, and base, and that the laborer, equally for his own good and for the welfare of the State, ought to be enslaved. The white laboring man, whether native or foreigner, is not enslaved only because he cannot as yet be reduced to bondage.

You need not be told now that the slave system is the older of the two and that once it was universal. The emancipation of our own ancestors, Caucasians and Europeans as they were, hardly dates beyond a period of five hundred years. The great melioration of human society which modern times exhibit is mainly due to the incomplete substitution of the system of voluntary labor for the old one of servile labor which has already taken place. This African slave system is one which, in its origin and its growth, has been altogether foreign from the habits of the races which colonized these States and established civilization here. It was introduced on this new continent as an engine of conquest and for the establishment of monarchical power by the Portuguese and the Spaniards, and was rapidly extended by them all over South America, Central America, Louisiana, and Mexico. Its legitimate fruits are seen in the poverty, imbecility, and anarchy which now pervade all Portuguese and Spanish America.

The free labor system is of German extraction, and it was established in our country by emigrants from Sweden, Holland, Germany, Great Britain, and Ireland. We justly ascribe to its influences the strength, wealth, greatness, intelligence, and freedom which the whole American people now enjoy. One of the chief elements of the value of human life is freedom in the pursuit of happiness. The slave system is not only intolerable, unjust, and inhuman toward the laborer, whom, only because he is a laborer, it loads down with chains and converts into merchandise, but is scarcely less severe upon the freeman, to whom, only because he is a laborer from necessity, it denies facilities for employment and whom it expels from the community because it cannot enslave and convert him into merchandise also. It is necessarily improvident and ruinous because, as a general truth, communities prosper and flourish, or droop and decline in just the degree that they practice or neglect to practice the primary duties of justice and humanity. The free labor system conforms to the divine law of equality which is written in the hearts and consciences of men, and therefore is always and everywhere beneficent.

The slave system is one of constant danger, distrust, suspicion, and watchfulness. It debases those whose toil alone can produce wealth and resources for defense to the lowest degree of which human nature is capable - to guard against mutiny and insurrection - and thus wastes energies which otherwise might be employed in national development and aggrandizement.

Russia yet maintains slavery and is a despotism. Most of the other European States have abolished slavery and adopted the system of free labor. It was the antagonistic political tendencies of the two systems which the first Napoleon was contemplating when he predicted that Europe would ultimately be either all Cossack or all republican. Never did human sagacity utter a more pregnant truth. The two systems are at once perceived to be incongruous. But they are more than incongruous - they are incompatible. They never have permanently existed together in one country and they never can. It would be easy to demonstrate this impossibility from the irreconcilable contrast between their great principles and characteristics. But the experience of mankind has conclusively established it.

Slavery, as I have already intimated, existed in every State in Europe. Free labor has supplanted it everywhere except in Russia and Turkey. State necessities developed in modern times are now obliging even those two nations to encourage and employ free labor; and already, despotic as they are, we find them engaged in abolishing slavery. In the United States slavery came into collision with free labor at the close of the last century, and fell before it in New England, New York, New Jersey, and Pennsylvania, but triumphed over it effectually and excluded it for a period yet undetermined, from Virginia, the Carolinas, and Georgia. Indeed, so incompatible are the two systems that every new State which is organized within our ever-extending domain makes its first political act a choice of the one and the exclusion of the other, even at the cost of civil war if necessary. The slave States, without law, at the last national election successfully forbade, within their own limits, even the casting of votes for a candidate for President of the United States supposed to be favorable to the establishment of the free labor system in new States.

Hitherto the two systems have existed in different States, but side by side within the American Union. This has happened because the Union is a confederation of States. But in another aspect the United States constitute only one nation. Increase of population, which is filling the States out to their very borders, together with a new and extended network of railroads and other avenues, and an internal commerce which daily becomes more intimate, is rapidly bringing the States into a higher and more perfect social unity or consolidation. Thus these antagonistic systems are continually coming into closer contact and collision results.

Shall I tell you what this collision means? They who think that it is accidental, unnecessary, the work of interested or fanatical agitators, and therefore ephemeral, mistake the case altogether. It is an irrepressible conflict between opposing and enduring forces, and it means that the United States must and will, sooner or later, become either entirely a slaveholding nation or entirely a free labor nation. Either the cotton and rice fields of South Carolina and the sugar plantations of Louisiana will ultimately be tilled by free labor, and Charleston and New Orleans become marts for legitimate merchandise alone, or else the rye fields and wheat fields of Massachusetts and New York must again be surrendered by their farmers to slave culture and to the production of slaves, and Boston and New York become once more markets for trade in the bodies and souls of men.

It is the failure to apprehend this great truth that induces so many unsuccessful attempts at final compromise between the slave and free States, and it is the existence of this great fact that renders all such pretended compromises, when made, vain and ephemeral. Startling as this saying may appear to you, fellow citizens, it is by no means an original or even a modern one. Our forefathers knew it to be true, and unanimously acted upon it when they framed the Constitution of the United States. They regarded the existence of the servile system in so many of the States with sorrow and shame, which they openly confessed, and they looked upon the collision between them, which was then just revealing itself, and which we are now accustomed to deplore, with favor and hope. They knew that either the one or the other system must exclusively prevail.

Unlike too many of those who in modern time invoke their authority, they had a choice between the two. They preferred the system of free labor, and they determined to organize the government and so to direct its activity that that system should surely and certainly prevail. For this purpose, and no other, they based the whole structure of government broadly on the principle that all men are created equal, and therefore free - little dreaming that within the short period of one hundred years their descendants would bear to be told by any orator, however popular, that the utterance of that principle was merely a rhetorical rhapsody, or by any judge, however venerated, that it was attended by mental reservations which rendered it hypocritical and false. By the Ordinance of 1787 they dedicated all of the national domain not yet polluted by slavery to free labor immediately, thenceforth, and forever, while by the new Constitution and laws they invited foreign free labor from all lands under the sun, and interdicted the importation of African slave labor, at all times, in all places, and under all circumstances whatsoever. It is true that they necessarily and wisely modified this policy of freedom by leaving it to the several States, affected as they were by differing circumstances, to abolish slavery in their own way and at their own pleasure, instead of confiding that duty to Congress, and that they secured to the slave States, while yet retaining the system of slavery, a three-fifths representation of slaves in the federal government, until they should find themselves able to relinquish it with safety. But the very nature of these modifications fortifies my position - that the fathers knew that the two systems could not endure within the Union, and expected that within a short period slavery would disappear forever. Moreover, in order that these modifications might not altogether defeat their grand design of a republic maintaining universal equality, they provided that two-thirds of the States might amend the Constitution.

The very Constitution of the Democratic party commits it to execute all the designs of the slaveholders, whatever they may be. It is not a party of the whole Union - of all the free States and of all the slave States; nor yet is it a party of the free States in the North and in the Northwest; but it is a sectional and local party, having practically its seat within the slave States and counting its constituency chiefly and almost exclusively there. Of all its representatives in Congress and in the electoral colleges, two-thirds uniformly come from these States. Its great element of strength lies in the vote of the slaveholders, augmented by the representation of three-fifths of the slaves. Deprive the Democratic party of this strength and it would be a helpless and hopeless minority, incapable of continued organization. The Democratic party, being thus local and sectional, acquires new strength from the admission of every new slave State and loses relatively by the admission of every new free State into the Union.

Afterward

William Seward lost the 1860 Republican Presidential nomination to Abraham Lincoln. He served as U.S. Secretary of State in both the Lincoln and Johnson Cabinets. In 1867 he negotiated *Seward's Treaty*, the purchase of Alaska.

William Seward died on October 10, 1872.

Selected Reading

Baker, George E., Editor, *The Life of William H. Seward*, 1855.

Bancroft, Frederic, *The Life of William H. Seward*, 1967.

Hale, Edward E., Jr., *William H. Seward*, 1910.

Lothrop, Thornton K., *William Henry Seward*, 1899.

Paolino, Ernest N., *The Foundations of the American Empire: William Henry Seward and U.S. Foreign Policy*, 1973.

Seward, William H., *Autobiography of William H. Seward*, 1877.

Taylor, John M., *William Henry Seward: Lincoln's Right Hand*, 1991.

Van Deusen, Glyndon G., *William Henry Seward*, 1967.

Elizabeth Cady Stanton
Declaration Of Sentiments
July 16, 1848

*The strongest reason why we ask for woman a voice in the government
is because of her birthright to self-sovereignty.*
   - Elizabeth Cady Stanton, *The Solitude of Self* (1892)

Elizabeth Cady Stanton, one of America's foremost *New
Women*, as feminists were then called, was born on November 12, 1815 in Johnstown, New York, the daughter of
Daniel and Margaret (Livingston) Cady. In 1840 Elizabeth
Cady married Henry Stanton, a leader of the American
Anti-Slavery Society. While attending the 1840 World Anti-
Slavery Convention in London, England, she was introduced to the most famous *New Woman* of her time, Lucretia
Mott. At the Convention the women delegates from
America, including Stanton and Mott, were denied participation and expelled from the seats they had been elected to
fill. Denied a role in the male-dominated Anti-Slavery
movement, Stanton, *outraged, humiliated and chagrined*, proposed to Lucretia Mott that they turn their efforts towards
Women's Rights - *As we walked, arm in arm, we resolved to hold
a convention as soon as we returned home, and to form a society to
advocate the rights of women.* Stanton, who was the mother of
seven children born between 1842 and 1859, dedicated her
life to obtaining equal rights for women.

On July 16, 1848, the First Women's Rights Convention was
held in Seneca Falls, New York. At the filled-to-over-
capacity Wesleyan Chapel, Elizabeth Cady Stanton told the
assembled women, *We have met here today to discuss our rights
and wrongs, civil and political.* Taking her theme from the Declaration of Independence, and including the same number
of enumerated grievances - eighteen - Elizabeth Cady
Stanton delivered this landmark speech, *Declaration Of Sentiments.*

When, in the course of human events, it becomes necessary for one portion of the family of man to assume among the people of the earth a position different from that which they have hitherto occupied, but one to which the laws of nature and of nature's God entitle them, a decent respect to the opinions of mankind requires that they should declare the causes that impel them to such a course.

We hold these truths to be self-evident - that all men and women are created equal; that they are endowed by their Creator with certain inalienable rights; that among these are life, liberty, and the pursuit of happiness; that to secure these rights governments are instituted, deriving their just powers from the consent of the governed. Whenever any form of government becomes destructive of these ends, it is the right of those who suffer from it to refuse allegiance to it, and to insist upon the institution of a new government, laying its foundation on such principles, and organizing its powers in such form, as to them shall seem most likely to effect their safety and happiness. Prudence indeed will dictate that governments long established should not be changed for light and transient causes, and accordingly all experience hath shown that mankind are more disposed to suffer, while evils are sufferable, than to right themselves by abolishing the forms to which they were accustomed. But when a long train of abuses and usurpations, pursuing invariably the same object, evinces a design to reduce them under absolute despotism, it is their duty to throw off such government, and to provide new guards for their future security. Such has been the patient sufferance of the women under this government, and such is now the necessity which constrains them to demand the equal station to which they are entitled.

The history of mankind is a history of repeated injuries and usurpations on the part of man toward woman, having in direct object the establishment of an absolute tyranny over her. To prove this, let facts be submitted to a candid world.

He has never permitted her to exercise her inalienable right to the elective franchise.

He has compelled her to submit to laws, in the formation of which she had no voice.

He has withheld from her rights which are given to the most ignorant and degraded men - both natives and foreigners.

Having deprived her of this first right of a citizen, the elective franchise, thereby leaving her without representation in the halls of legislation, he has oppressed her on all sides.

He has made her, if married, in the eye of the law, civilly dead.

He has taken from her all right in property, even to the wages she earns.

He has made her, morally, an irresponsible being, as she can commit many crimes with impunity, provided they be done in the presence of her husband. In the covenant of marriage, she is compelled to promise obedience to her husband, he becoming, to all intents and purposes, her master - the law giving him power to deprive her of her liberty, and to administer chastisement.

He has so framed the laws of divorce as to what shall be the proper causes, and in case of separation, to whom the guardianship of the children shall be given, as to be wholly regardless of the happiness of women - the law, in all cases, going upon a false supposition of the supremacy of man, and giving all power into his hands.

After depriving her of all rights as a married woman, if single, and the owner of property, he has taxed her to support a government which recognizes her only when her property can be made profitable to it.

He has monopolized nearly all the profitable employments, and from those she is permitted to follow, she receives but a scanty remuneration. He closes against her all the avenues to wealth and distinction which he considers most honorable to himself. As a teacher of theology, medicine, or law, she is not known.

He has denied her the facilities for obtaining a thorough education, all colleges being closed against her.

He allows her in Church, as well as State, but a subordinate position, claiming Apostolic authority for her exclusion from the ministry, and, with some exceptions, from any public participation in the affairs of the Church.

He has created a false public sentiment by giving to the world a different code of morals for men and women, by which moral delinquencies which exclude women from society are not only tolerated, but deemed of little account in man.

He has usurped the prerogative of Jehovah himself, claiming it as his right to assign for her a sphere of action, when that belongs to her conscience and to her God.

He has endeavored, in every way that he could, to destroy her confidence in her own powers, to lessen her self-respect, and to make her willing to lead a dependent and abject life.

Now, in view of this entire disfranchisement of one-half the people of this country, their social and religious degradation - in view of the unjust laws above mentioned, and because women do feel themselves aggrieved, oppressed, and fraudulently deprived of their most sacred rights - we insist that they have immediate admission to all the rights and privileges which belong to them as citizens of the United States.

In entering upon the great work before us, we anticipate no small amount of misconception, misrepresentation, and ridicule, but we shall use every instrumentality within our power to effect our object. We shall employ agents, circulate tracts, petition the State and National legislatures, and endeavor to enlist the pulpit and the press in our behalf. We hope this Convention will be followed by a series of Conventions embracing every part of the country.

Afterward

In 1920, eighteen years after Stanton's death, the Nineteenth *Woman's Suffrage* Amendment was adopted - *The right of citizens of the United States to vote shall not be denied or abridged on account of sex.*

Elizabeth Cady Stanton died on October 26, 1902.

Selected Reading

Banner, Lois, *Elizabeth Cady Stanton: A Radical for Woman's Rights*, 1980.

Griffith, Elisabeth, *In Her Own Right: The Life of Elizabeth Cady Stanton*, 1940.

Lutz, Alma, *Created Equal: A Biography of Elizabeth Cady Stanton*, 1984.

Stanton, Elizabeth Cady, *Eighty Years and More: Reminiscences, 1815-1897*, 1898.

Tecumseh, War Chief of the Shawnee
Broken American Promises
August 12, 1810

If it were not for his proximity to the United States Tecumseh could perhaps have been the founder of an Indian empire that would have rivaled Mexico or Peru in glory. **- William Henry Harrison**

Tecumseh (*The Shooting Star*) was born in 1768 in the village of Piqua (near present-day Springfield, Ohio). His mother was Methoataske. His father was Puckeshinwa, a Shawnee War Chief in both the French and Indian War and the Pontiac Rebellion. The Ohio Valley was the home of several native American tribes, including the Shawnee. A Tribal Alliance had for two generations united to fight white settlement in the Ohio Valley, first against the French and then against the British. When the United States obtained the Northwest Territory (present-day Ohio, Indiana, Illinois, Michigan, Wisconsin, and Minnesota) from Great Britain in 1783, the enemy became the Americans.

When his father and older brother were killed in battle, leadership of the Shawnee fell to Tecumseh. On August 20, 1794, at the Battle of Fallen Timbers, U.S. General *Mad* Anthony Wayne, sent by President Washington to subdue the native tribes, decisively defeated the Tribal Alliance. The Indian leaders, without Tecumseh, then signed the first of many treaties selling millions of acres to the United States. Tecumseh refused to recognize the validity of these treaties and demanded that the war go on - *Have we not courage enough to defend our country and maintain our ancient independence?*

On August 12, 1810, at a Peace Summit held at Vincennes, Indiana Territory, called by the Territory's Governor William Henry Harrison, Tecumseh gave this landmark speech, *Broken American Promises.*

Brother, I wish you to give me close attention, because I think you do not clearly understand. I want to speak to you about promises that the Americans have made.

You recall the time when the Jesus Indians of the Delawares lived near the Americans, and had confidence in their promises of friendship, and thought they were secure, yet the Americans murdered all the men, women, and children, even as they prayed to Jesus?

The same promises were given to the Shawnee one time. It was at Fort Finney, where some of my people were forced to make a treaty. Flags were given to my people, and they were told they were now the children of the Americans. We were told, if any white people mean to harm you, hold up these flags and you will then be safe from all danger. We did this in good faith. But what happened? Our beloved chief Moluntha stood with the American flag in front of him and that very peace treaty in his hand, but his head was chopped by a American officer, and that American officer was never punished.

Brother, after such bitter events, can you blame me for placing little confidence in the promises of Americans? That happened before the Treaty of Greenville. When they buried the tomahawk at Greenville, the Americans said they were our new fathers, not the British anymore, and would treat us well. Since that treaty, here is how the Americans have treated us well - they have killed many Shawnee, many Winnebagoes, many Miamis, many Delawares, and have taken land from them. When they killed them, no American ever was punished, not one.

It is you, the Americans, by such bad deeds, who push the red men to do mischief. You do not want unity among the tribes, and you destroy it. You try to make differences between them. We, their leaders, wish them to unite and consider their land the common property of all, but you try to keep them from this. You separate the tribes and deal with them that way, one by one, and advise them not to come into this union. Your states have set an example of forming a union . . . ; why should you censure the Indians for following that example?

But, brother, I mean to bring all the tribes together, in spite of you, and until I have finished, I will not go to visit your President. Maybe I will when I have finished, maybe. The reason I tell you this - you want, by making your distinctions of Indian tribes and allotting to each a particular tract of land, to set them against each other, and thus to weaken us.
You never see an Indian come, do you, and endeavor to make the white people divide up?

You are always driving the red people this way! At last you will drive them into the Great Lake, where they can neither stand nor walk.

Brother, you ought to know what you are doing to the Indians. Is it by the direction of the President you make these distinctions? It is a very bad thing, and we do not like it. Since my residence at Tippecanoe, we have tried to level all distinctions, to destroy village chiefs, by whom all such mischief is done. It is they who sell our lands to the Americans. Brother, these lands that were sold and the goods that were given for them were done by only a few. The Treaty of Fort Wayne was made through the threats of Winnemac, but in the future we are going to punish those chiefs who propose to sell the land.

The only way to stop this evil is for all the red men to unite in claiming an equal right in the land. That is how it was at first, and should be still, for the land never was divided, but was for the use of everyone. Any tribe could go to an empty land and make a home there. And if they left, another tribe could come there and make a home. No groups among us have a right to sell, even to one another, and surely not to outsiders who want all, and will not do with less.

Sell a country! Why not sell the air, the clouds, and the Great Sea, as well as the earth? Did not the Great Good Spirit make them all for the use of his children?

Brother, I was glad to hear what you told us. You said that if we could prove that the land was sold by people who had no right to sell it, you would restore it. I will prove that those who did sell did not own it. Did they have a deed? A title? No! You say those prove someone owns land. Those chiefs only spoke a claim, and so you pretended to believe their claim, only because you wanted the land. But the many tribes with me will not agree with those claims. They have never had a title to sell, and we agree this proves you could not buy it from them. If the land is not given back to us, you will see, when we return to our homes from here, how it will be settled. It will be like this - we shall have a great council, at which all tribes will be present. We shall show to those who sold that they had no rights to the claim they set up, and we shall see what will be done to those chiefs who did sell the land to you. I am not alone in this determination; it is the determination of all the warriors and red people who listen to me. Brother, I now wish you to listen to me. If you do not wipe out that treaty, it will seem that you wish me to kill all the chiefs who sold the land! I tell you so because I am authorized by all tribes to do so! I am the head of them all! All my warriors will meet together with me in two or three moons from now. Then I will call for those chiefs who sold you this land, and we shall know what to do with them. If you do not restore the land, you will have had a hand in killing them!

I am Shawnee! I am a warrior! My forefathers were warriors. From them I took only my birth into this world. From my tribe I take nothing. I am the maker of my own destiny! And of that I might make the destiny of my red people, of our nation, as great as I conceive to in my mind, when I think of Weshemoneto, who rules this universe! I would not then have to come to Governor Harrison and ask him to tear up this treaty and wipe away the marks upon the land. No! I would say to him, *Sir, you may return to your own country!* The being within me hears the voice of the ages, which tells me that once, always, and until lately, there were no white men on all this island, that it then belonged to the red men, children of the same parents, placed on it by the Great Good Spirit who made them, to keep it, to traverse it, to enjoy its yield, and to people it with the same race. Once they were a happy race! Now they are made miserable by the white people, who are never contented but are always coming in! You do this always, after promising not to anyone, yet you ask us to have confidence in your promises. How can we have confidence in the white people? When Jesus Christ came upon the earth, you killed him - the son of your own God - you nailed him up! You thought he was dead, but you were mistaken. And only after you thought you killed him did you worship him, and start killing those who would not worship him. What kind of a people is this for us to trust?

Now, Brother, everything I have said to you is the truth, as Weshemoneto has inspired me to speak only truth to you. I have declared myself freely to you about my intentions. And I want to know your intentions. I want to know what you are going to do about the taking of our land. I want to hear you say that you understand now, and will wipe out that pretended treaty, so that the tribes can be at peace with each other, as you pretend you want them to be. Tell me, brother. I want to know now.

Afterward

On November 6, 1811, American forces under William Henry Harrison defeated Tecumseh's warriors at the Battle of Tippecanoe (present-day LaFayette, Indiana).

Tecumseh was killed in battle on October 5, 1813.

Selected Reading

Colton, George H., *Tecumseh*, 1842.

Cooke, David C., *Tecumseh, Destiny's Warrior*, 1959.

Drake, Benjamin, *Life of Tecumseh*, 1988.

Eckert, Allan W., *A Sorrow in Our Heart: The Life of Tecumseh*, 1992.

Edmunds, R. David, *Tecumseh and the Quest for Indian Leadership*, 1984.

Gutteridge, Don, *Tecumseh*, 1976.

Oskison, John M., *Tecumseh and His Times: The Story of a Great Indian*, 1938.

Raymond, Ethel T., *Tecumseh: A Chronicle of the Last Great Leader of His People*, 1920.

Shorto, Russell, *Tecumseh and the Dream of an American Indian Nation*, 1989.

Stefoff, Rebecca, *Tecumseh and the Shawnee Confederation*, 1998.

Sugden, John, *Tecumseh: A Life*, 1998.

Tucker, Glenn, *Tecumseh: Vision of Glory*, 1956.

Henry David Thoreau
Walking West
April 23, 1851

*My journal is that of me which would else spill over and run to waste,
gleaning from the field which in action I reap. I must not live for it,
but in it.*   **- Thoreau's** *Journal* **, February 8, 1841**

On October 22, 1837, Henry David Thoreau, then twenty
years old, made his first entry into his *Journal.* Over the next
twenty-four years of his life, Thoreau wrote almost two
million words on his experiences and reflections.

Henry David Thoreau was born was born on July 12, 1817
in Concord, Massachusetts, the son of John and Cynthia
(Dunbar) Thoreau. At Harvard College, he studied litera-
ture under Edward Channing, the teacher of Ralph Waldo
Emerson, James Russell Lowell, Oliver Wendell Holmes, Sr.,
Edward Everett Hale, and Richard Henry Dana.

Following his friend Emerson, Thoreau became a writer,
and is best known now for his books, *A Week on the Concord
and Merrimack Rivers* and *Walden.* He was best known then as
a lecturer. Thoreau traveled, mostly by foot, throughout
New England, and delivered philosophical, literary, and nature lectures, drawn from his *Journal,* for a fee of twenty
dollars. His lectures became so popular that Thoreau was in
constant demand. Some of the most popular were *Society*
(April 11, 1838), *The Ancient Poets* (November 29, 1843), *The
Concord River* (March 25, 1845), *A History of Myself*
(February 10, 1847), *The Maine Woods* (January 5, 1848), *Civil
Disobedience* (January 26, 1848), *Economy* (November 22,
1848), *Walden Pond* (January 3, 1849), *Life In The Woods*
(March 21, 1849), and *Cape Cod* (January 23, 1850).

On April 23, 1851, before an audience of admirers gathered
at Concord's Lyceum, Henry David Thoreau delivered this
lecture, his personal favorite, *Walking West.*

Henry David Thoreau

What is it that makes it so hard sometimes to determine whither we will walk? I believe that there is a subtle magnetism in nature which, if we unconsciously yield to it, will direct us aright. It is not indifferent to us which way we walk. There is a right way; but we are very liable from heedlessness and stupidity to take the wrong one. We would fain take that walk never yet taken by us through this actual world, which is perfectly symbolical of the path which we love to travel in the interior and ideal world; and sometimes, no doubt, we find it difficult to choose our direction, because it does not yet exist distinctly in our idea.

When I go out of the house for a walk, uncertain as yet whither I will bend my steps, and submit myself to my instinct to decide for me, I find, strange and whimsical as it may seem, that I finally and inevitably settle southwest, toward some particular wood or meadow or deserted pasture or hill in that direction. My needle is slow to settle - varies a few degrees, and does not always point due southwest, it is true, and it has good authority for this variation, but it always settles between west and south-southwest. The future lies that way to me, and the earth seems more unexhausted and richer on that side. The outline which would bound my walks would be not a circle but a parabola, or rather like one of those cometary orbits which have been thought to be nonreturning curves, in this case opening westward, in which my house occupies the place of the sun.

I turn round and round, irresolute, sometimes for a quarter of an hour, until I decide, for a thousandth time, that I will walk into the southwest or west. Eastward I go only by force; but westward I go free. Thither no business leads me. It is hard for me to believe that I shall find fair landscapes or sufficient wildness and freedom behind the eastern horizon. I am not excited by the prospect of a walk thither;

but I believe that the forest which I see in the western horizon stretches uninterruptedly toward the setting sun, and there are no towns nor cities in it of enough consequence to disturb me.

Let me live where I will - on this side is the city, on that the wilderness - and ever I am leaving the city more and more and withdrawing into the wilderness. I should not lay so much stress on this fact if I did not believe that something like this is the prevailing tendency of my countrymen. I must walk toward Oregon and not toward Europe. And that way the nation is moving, and I may say that mankind progress from east to west. Within a few years we have witnessed the phenomenon of a southeastward migration, in the settlement of Australia; but this affects us as a retrograde movement, and, judging from the moral and physical character of the first generation of Australians, has not yet proved a successful experiment. The Eastern Tartars think that there is nothing west beyond Tibet. *The world ends there,* say they; *beyond there is nothing but a shoreless sea.* It is unmitigated East where they live.

We go eastward to realize history and study the works of art and literature, retracing the steps of the race; we go westward as into the future, with a spirit of enterprise and adventure. The Atlantic is a Lethean stream, in our passage over which we have had an opportunity to forget the Old World and its institutions. If we do not succeed this time, there is perhaps one more chance for the race left before it arrives on the banks of the Styx, and that is in the Lethe of the Pacific, which is three times as wide.

Afterward

Henry David Thoreau died on May 6, 1862. Ralph Waldo Emerson delivered this eulogy,

Henry David Thoreau

The scale on which his studies proceeded was so large as to require longevity, and we were the less prepared for his sudden disappearance. The country knows not yet, or in the least part, how great a son it has lost. It seems an injury that he should leave in the midst his broken task, which none else can finish, a kind of indignity to so noble a soul, that it should depart out of Nature before yet he has been really shown to his peers for what he is. But he, at least, is content. His soul was made for the noblest society; he had in a short life exhausted the capabilities of this world; wherever there is knowledge, wherever there is virtue, wherever there is beauty, he will find a home.

Selected Reading

Canby, Henry, *Thoreau*, 1939.
Harding, Walter, *The Days of Henry Thoreau*, 1962.
Krutch, Joseph, *Henry David Thoreau*, 1948.
Sanborn, Franklin, *The Life of Henry David Thoreau*, 1916.
Van Doren, Mark, *Henry David Thoreau*, 1916.

Sojourner Truth
A'n't I A Woman?
June 21, 1851

A tall, gaunt black woman in a gray dress and white turban marched deliberately into the church, walking with the air of a queen up the aisle. She moved slowly and solemnly to the pulpit. Every eye was fixed on this most Amazon form, which stood nearly six feet high, head erect and eyes piercing the upper air like in a dream. At her first word there was a profound hush. She spoke in deep tones, which, though not loud, reached every ear in the house, and away through the throng at the doors and windows. **- Frances Gage, June 21, 1851**

The African-American woman who re-christened herself Sojouner Truth was born about 1797 in Ulster County, New York. Taken from her parents when she was nine, *Isabella* (her slave name) became the property of several slaveholders before being sold for the last time, in 1810, for $175, to Ulster County's Dumont family. In about 1815, she married another Dumont slave and had five children.

Isabella became a free woman on July 4, 1827, when New York State abolished slavery. On June 1, 1843, in answer to the call of *The Holy Spirit* that she *testify against wickedness*, she changed her name to *Sojourner Truth* and became a traveling evangelist preacher, famous as a forceful and dynamic speaker for the anti-slavery and women's rights movements. Two books, *The Narrative of Sojouner Truth* (her autobiography, published in 1850) and Harriet Beecher Stowe's *Sojouner Truth: The Libyan Sibyl* (published in 1863), made her nationally famous.

Sojouner Truth's *A'n't I A Woman* was delivered at the Women's Rights Convention held in Akron, Ohio's Stone Church in 1851. This eyewitness report of Sojouner Truth's speech, along with [a bracketed commentary] was taken down that day by women's suffrage activist Frances Gage.

Well, children, where there is so much racket there must be somethin' out o' kilter. I think that 'twixt the niggers of the South and the women at the North, all talkin' 'bout rights, the white men will be in a fix pretty soon. But what's all this here talkin' 'bout?

That man over there says that woman needs to be helped into carriages, and lifted over ditches, and to have the best place everywhere. Nobody ever helps me into carriages, or over mud puddles, or gives me any best place! [And raising herself to her full height, and her voice to a pitch like rolling thunder, she asked,] And a'n't I a woman? Look at me! Look at my arm! [And she bared her right arm to the shoulder, showing her tremendous muscular power.] I have plowed, and planted, and gathered into barns, and no man could head me! And a'n't I a woman? I could work as much and eat as much as a man - when I could get it - and bear the lash as well! And a'n't I a woman? I have borne thirteen children, and seen 'em mos' all sold off to slavery, and when I cried out with my mother's grief, none but Jesus heard me! And a'n't I a woman?

Then they talks 'bout this thing in the head - what this they call it? [*Intellect*, whispered some one near.] That's it, honey. What's that got to do with women's rights or nigger's rights? If my cup won't hold but a pint, and yours holds a quart, wouldn't you be mean not to let me have my little half-measure full? [And she pointed her significant finger, and sent a keen glance at the minister who had made the argument. The cheering was long and loud.]

Then that little man in black there, he say women can't have as much rights as men, cause Christ wan't a woman! Where did your Christ come from? [Rolling thunder couldn't have stilled that crowd, as did those deep, wonderful tones, as she stood there with outstretched arms and eyes of fire.

Raising her voice still louder, she repeated,] Where did your Christ come from? From God and a woman! Man had nothin' to do with Him. [Oh, what a rebuke that was to that little man.]

[Turning again to another objector, she took up the defense of Mother Eve. I cannot follow her through it all. It was pointed, and witty, and solemn - eliciting at almost every sentence deafening applause - and she ended by asserting,] If the first woman God ever made was strong enough to turn the world upside down all alone, these women together [and she glanced her eye over the platform] ought to be able to turn it back, and get it right side up again! And now they is asking to do it, the men better let 'em. [Long-continued cheering greeted this.] 'Bliged to you for hearin' on me, and now old Sojourner han't got nothin' more to say.

Afterward
Susan B. Anthony summed up Sojourner Truth's influence on the women's and civil rights movements, writing,

> *She combined in herself as an individual the two most hated elements of humanity. She was black, and she was a woman. All the insults that could be cast upon color and sex were together hurled at her, but there she stood, calm and dignified, a grand wise woman who, with deep insight, could penetrate the very soul of the universe about her.*

Sojouner Truth died on November 26, 1883.

Selected Reading
Bernard, Jacqueline, *Journey Towards Freedom: The Story of Sojourner Truth*, 1967.

Ortiz, Victoria, *Sojourner Truth: A Self-Made Woman*, 1989.

Painter, Nell, *Sojourner Truth: A Life, A Symbol*, 1996.

Truth, Sojourner, *Narrative Of Sojourner Truth*, 1850.

Nat Turner
The Confession Of Nat Turner
November 1, 1831

The calm, deliberate composure with which he spoke of his late deeds and intentions, the expression of his fiend-like face when excited by enthusiasm, still bearing the stains of blood of helpless innocence about him; clothed with rags and covered with chains; yet daring to raise his manacled hands to heaven, with a spirit soaring above the attributes of man; I looked on him and my blood curdled in my veins.
-Thomas Gray, Attorney For Nat Turner (1831)

Nat Turner was born into slavery on October 2, 1800 on a plantation in Southampton County, Virginia. Sold several times in his life - the last price paid for him was $400 - he was in 1831 the property of slaveowners Joseph and Sally Travis. Turner had as a child been taught to read the Bible. His study of the Bible led him to became a *fire and brimstone* preacher in Southampton County's black churches.

On May 12, 1828, Turner experienced a vision - *I heard a loud noise in the heavens, and the Spirit instantly appeared to me and said the Serpent was loosened, . . . that I should take it on and fight against the Serpent, for the time was fast approaching when the first should be last and the last should be first.* Turner believed this vision instructed him to lead a slave revolt. He began to secretly recruit and arm followers. Two slave-led revolts in Turner's lifetime - Gabriel Prosser's in 1800 and Denmark Vesey's in 1822 - had both ended in failure. Turner, believing his plan divinely inspired, thought his would succeed.

On Sunday, August 21 and Monday, August 22, 1831, Turner and his 75 followers killed 51 whites, including the Travis family. The State Militia put down *Nat Turner's Rebellion* and Turner himself was captured. This landmark speech, *The Confession of Nat Turner*, dictated to his lawyer, was read at his trial on November 5, 1831.

You have asked me to give a history of the motives which induced me to undertake the late insurrection, as you call it. To do so I must go back to the days of my infancy, and even before I was born. I was thirty-one years of age the second of October last, and born the property of Benjamin Turner, of this county. In my childhood a circumstance occurred which made an indelible impression on my mind, and laid the groundwork of that enthusiasm, which has terminated so fatally to many, both white and black, and for which I am about to atone at the gallows. It is here necessary to relate this circumstance, trifling as it may seem - it was the commencement of that belief which has grown with time, and even now, sir, in this dungeon, helpless and forsaken as I am, I cannot divest myself of. Being at play with other children, when three or four years old, I was telling them something which, my mother overhearing, said it had happened before I was born. I stuck by my story, however, and related some things which went, in her opinion, to confirm it; others being called on were greatly astonished, knowing that these things had happened, and caused them to say in my hearing, I surely would be a prophet, as the Lord had shown me things that had happened before my birth. And my father and mother strengthened me in this, my first impression, saying in my presence, I was intended for some great purpose. . . .

Having soon discovered to be great, I must appear so, and therefore studiously avoided mixing in society, and wrapped myself in mystery, devoting my time to fasting and prayer. By this time, having arrived to man's estate, and hearing the scriptures commented on at meetings, I was struck with that particular passage which says, *Seek ye the kingdom of Heaven and all things shall be added unto you.* I reflected much on this passage, and prayed daily for light on this subject. As I was praying one day at my plow, the spirit spoke to me, saying, *Seek ye the kingdom of Heaven and all things shall be added unto you.*

. . . . I was greatly astonished, and for two years prayed continually, whenever my duty would permit, and then again I had the same revelation, which fully confirmed me in the impression that I was ordained for some great purpose in the hands of the Almighty.

. . . . Now finding I had arrived to man's estate, and was a slave, and these revelations being made known to me, I began to direct my attention to this great object, to fulfill the purpose for which, by this time, I felt assured I was intended. Knowing the influence I had obtained over the minds of my fellow servants, not by the means of conjuring and such like tricks, for to them I always spoke of such things with contempt - but by the communion of the Spirit whose revelations I often communicated to them, and they believed and said my wisdom came from God - I now began to prepare them for my purpose, by telling them something was about to happen that would terminate in fulfilling the great promise that had been made to me. . . . And about this time I had a vision, and I saw white spirits and black spirits engaged in battle, and the sun was darkened, the thunder rolled in the Heavens, and blood flowed in streams, and I heard a voice saying, *Such is your luck, such you are called to see, and let it come rough or smooth, you must surely bear it.* I now withdrew myself, as much as my situation would permit, from the intercourse of my fellow servants, for the avowed purpose of serving the Spirit more fully, and it appeared to me, and reminded me of the things it had already shown me, and that it would then reveal to me the knowledge of the elements, the revolution of the planets, the operation of tides, and changes of the seasons. After this revelation in the year 1825, and the knowledge of the elements being made known to me, I sought more than ever to obtain true holiness before the great day of judgment should appear, and then I began to receive the true knowledge of faith. And from the first steps of righteousness until the last, was I made perfect; and the Holy Ghost was with me, and said, *Behold me as I stand in the Heavens,* and I looked and saw the forms of men in different attitudes, and there were lights in the sky to which the children of darkness gave other names than what they really were, for they were lights of the Savior's hands, stretched forth from east to west, even as they were extended on the cross on Calvary for the redemption of sinners. And I wondered greatly at these miracles, and prayed to be informed of a certainty of the meaning thereof, and shortly afterwards, while laboring in the field, I discovered drops of blood on the corn as though it were dew from heaven, and I communicated it to many, both white and black, in the neighborhood, and I then found on the leaves in the woods hieroglyphic characters, and numbers, with the forms of men in different attitudes, portrayed in blood, and representing the figures I had seen before in the heavens. And now the Holy Ghost had revealed itself to me, and made plain the miracles it had shown me. For as the blood of Christ had been shed on this earth, and had ascended to heaven for the salvation of sinners, and now was returning unto earth again in the form of dew, and as the leaves on the trees bore the impression of the figures I had seen in the heavens, it was plain to me that the Savior was about to lay down the yoke he had borne for the sins of men, and the great day of judgment was at hand. About this time I told these things to a white man (Etheldred T. Brantley), on whom it had a wonderful effect, and he ceased from his wickedness, and was attacked immediately with a cutaneous eruption, and blood oozed from the pores of his skin, and after praying and fasting nine days, he was healed, and the Spirit appeared to me again, and said, as the Savior had been baptized so should we be also, and when the white people would not let us be baptized by the church, we went down into the water together, in the sight of many who reviled us, and were baptized by the Spirit. After this I rejoiced greatly, and gave thanks to God. And on the twelfth of May, 1828, I heard a loud noise in the heavens, and the Spirit instantly appeared to me and said the Serpent was loosened, and Christ had laid down the yoke he had borne for the sins of men, and that I should take it on and fight against the Serpent, for the time was fast approaching when the first should be last and the last should be first.

. . . . [B]y signs in the heavens . . . it would be made known to me when I should commence the great work - and until the first sign appeared, I should conceal it from the knowledge of men. And on the appearance of the sign (the eclipse of the sun last February), I should arise and prepare myself, and slay my enemies with their own weapons. And immediately on the sign appearing in the heavens, the seal was removed from my lips, and I communicated the great work laid out before me to do, to four in whom I had the greatest confidence - Henry, Hark, Nelson, and Sam. It was intended by us to have begun the work of death on the fourth of July last. Many were the plans formed and rejected by us, and it affected my mind to such a degree that I fell sick, and the time passed without our coming to any determination how to commence. Still forming new schemes and rejecting them, when the sign appeared again, which determined me not to wait longer.

Since the commencement of 1830, I had been living with Mr. Joseph Travis, who was to me a kind master, and placed the greatest confidence in me; in fact, I had no cause to complain of his treatment of me. On Saturday evening, the twentieth of August, it was agreed between Henry, Hark, and myself to prepare a dinner the next day for the men we expected, and then to concert a plan, as we had not yet determined on any. Hark, on the following morning, brought a pig, and Henry brandy, and being joined by Sam, Nelson, Will, and Jack, they prepared in the woods a dinner, where, about three o'clock, I joined them.

. . . . I saluted them on coming up, and asked Will how he came to be there; he answered, his life was worth no more than others, and his liberty as dear to him; I asked him if he thought to obtain it. He said he would, or lose his life. This was enough to put him in full confidence. Jack, I knew, was only a tool in the hands of Hark; it was quickly agreed we should commence at home (Mr. J. Travis') on that night, and until we had armed and equipped ourselves, and gathered sufficient force, neither age nor sex was to be spared (which was invariably adhered to). We remained at the feast, until about two hours in the night, when we went to the house and found Austin; they all went to the cider press and drank except myself. On returning to the house, Hark went to the door with an ax, for the purpose of breaking it open, as we knew we were strong enough to murder the family, if they were awakened by the noise; but reflecting that it might create an alarm in the neighborhood, we determined to enter the house secretly, and murder them whilst sleeping. Hark got a ladder and set it against the chimney, on which I ascended, and hoisting a window, entered and came downstairs, unbarred the door, and removed the guns from their places. It was then observed that I must spill the first blood - on which, armed with a hatchet, and accompanied by Will, I entered my master's chamber; it being dark, I could not give a death blow; the hatchet glanced from his head, he sprang from the bed and called his wife. It was his last word - Will laid him dead with a blow of his ax, and Mrs. Travis shared the same fate, as she lay in bed. The murder of this family, five in number, was the work of a moment; not one of them awoke. There was a little infant sleeping in a cradle that was forgotten until we had left the house and gone some distance, when Henry and Will returned and killed it. We got here four guns that would shoot, and several old muskets, with a pound or two of powder. We remained some time at the barn, where we paraded; I formed them in a line as soldiers, and after carrying them through all the maneuvers I was master of, marched them off to Mr. Salathul Francis', about six hundred yards distant. Sam and Will went to the door and knocked. Mr. Francis asked who was there; Sam replied it was him, and he had a letter for him, on which he got up and came to the door; they immediately seized him, and dragging him out a little from the door, he was dispatched by repeated blows on the head; there was no other white person in the family. We started from there for Mrs. Reese's, maintaining the most perfect silence on our march. . . . Finding the door unlocked, we entered, and murdered Mrs. Reese in her bed, while sleeping; her son awoke, but it was only to sleep the sleep of death; he had only time to say who is that, and he was no more. From Mrs. Reese's we went to Mrs. Turner's, a mile distant, which we reached about sunrise, on Monday morning. Henry, Austin, and Sam went to the still, where, finding Mr. Peebles, Austin shot him, and the rest of us went to the house; as we approached, the family discovered us, and shut the door. Vain hope! Will, with one stroke of his ax, opened it, and we entered and found Mrs. Turner and Mrs. Newsome in the middle of a room, almost frightened to death. Will immediately killed Mrs. Turner, with one blow of his ax. I took Mrs. Newsome by the hand, and with the sword I had when I was apprehended, I struck her several blows over the head but, not being able to kill her, as the sword was dull, Will, turning around and discovering it, dispatched her also. A general destruction of property and search for money and ammunition always succeeded the murders. By this time my company amounted to fifteen, and nine men mounted, who started for Mrs. Whitehead's - the other six were to go through a byway to Mr. Bryant's, and rejoin us at Mrs. Whitehead's. As we approached the house we discovered Mr. Richard Whitehead standing in the cotton patch, near the lane fence; we called him over into the lane, and Will, the executioner, was near at hand, with his fatal ax, to send him to an untimely grave. As we pushed on to the house, I discovered someone run round the garden and, thinking it was some of the white family, I pursued them, but finding it was a servant girl belonging to the house, I returned to commence the work of death, but they whom I left had not been idle; all the family were already murdered, but Mrs. Whitehead and her daughter Margaret. As I came round to the door, I saw Will pulling Mrs. Whitehead out of the house, and at the step he nearly severed her head from her body with his broad ax. Miss Margaret, when I discovered her, had concealed herself in the corner, formed by the projection of the cellar cap from the house; on my approach she fled, but was soon overtaken, and after repeated blows with a sword, I killed her by a blow on the head with a fence rail. By this time, the six who had gone by Mr. Bryant's rejoined us, and informed me they had done the work of death assigned them. We again divided, part going to Mr. Richard Porter's, and from thence to Nathaniel Francis', the others to Mr. Howell Harris', and Mr. T. Doyle's. On my reaching Mr. Porter's, he had escaped with his family. I understood there that the alarm had already spread, and I immediately returned to bring up those sent to Mr. Doyle's and Mr. Harris', the party I left going on to Mr. Francis', having told them I would join them in that neighborhood. I met those sent to Mr. Doyle's and Mr. Harris' returning, having met Mr. Doyle on the road and killed him; and learning from some who joined them that Mr. Harris was from home, I immediately pursued the course taken by the party gone on before; but knowing they would complete the work of death and pillage at Mr. Francis' before I could get there, I went on to Mr. Peter Edwards', expecting to find them there, but they had been here also. I then went to Mr. John T. Barrow's; they had been here and murdered him. I pursued on their track to Captain Newit Harris', where I found the greater part mounted, and ready to start; the men now amounting to about forty shouted and hurraed as I rode up; some were in the yard, loading their guns, others drinking. They said Captain Harris and his family had escaped; the property in the house they destroyed, robbing him of money and other valuables. I ordered them to mount and march instantly; this was about nine or ten o'clock Monday morning. I proceeded to Mr. Levi Waller's, two or three miles distant. I took my station in the rear; as it was my object to carry terror and devastation wherever we went, I placed fifteen or twenty of the best armed and most to be relied on in front, who generally approached the houses as fast as their horses could run; this was for two purposes - to prevent their escape and strike terror to the inhabitants. On this account I never got to the houses, after leaving Mrs. Whitehead's, until the murders were committed, except in one case. I sometimes got in sight in time to see the work of death completed, viewed the mangled bodies as they lay, in silent satisfaction, and immediately started in quest of other victims. Having murdered Mrs. Waller and ten children, we started for Mr. William Williams' - having killed him and two little boys that were there; while engaged in this, Mrs. Williams fled and got some distance from the house, but she was pursued, overtaken, and compelled to get up behind one of the company, who brought her back and, after showing her the mangled body of her lifeless husband, she was told to get down and lay by his side, where she was shot dead. I then started for Mr.

Jacob Williams, where the family were murdered. Here we found a young man named Drury, who had come on business with Mr. Williams - he was pursued, overtaken and shot. Mrs. Vaughan was the next place visited - and after murdering the family here, I determined on starting for Jerusalem. Our number amounted now to fifty or sixty, all mounted and armed with guns, axes, swords, and clubs. On reaching Mr. James W. Parker's gate, immediately on the road leading to Jerusalem, and about three miles distant, it was proposed to me to call there, but I objected, as I knew he was gone to Jerusalem, and my object was to reach there as soon as possible; but, some of the men having relations at Mr. Parker's, it was agreed that they might call and get his people. I remained at the gate on the road, with seven or eight, the others going across the field to the house, about half a mile off. After waiting some time for them, I became impatient, and started to the house for them, and on our return we were met by a party of white men, who had pursued our blood-stained track, and who had fired on those at the gate, and dispersed them, which I knew nothing of, not having been at that time rejoined by any of them. Immediately on discovering the whites, I ordered my men to halt and form, as they appeared to be alarmed. The white men, eighteen in number, approached us in about one hundred yards, when one of them fired - this was against the positive orders of Captain Alexander P. Peete, who commanded, and who had directed the men to reserve their fire until within thirty paces. And I discovered about half of them retreating; I then ordered my men to fire and rush them; the few remaining stood their ground until we approached within fifty yards, when they fired and retreated. We pursued and overtook some of them who we thought we left dead - they were not killed - after pursuing them about two hundred yards, and rising a little hill, I discovered they were met by another party, and had halted, and were reloading their guns. This was a small party from Jerusalem who knew the negroes were in the field, and had just tied their horses to wait their return to the road, knowing that Mr. Parker and family were in Jerusalem, but knew nothing of the party that had gone in with Captain Peete; on hearing the firing, they immediately rushed to the spot and arrived just in time to arrest the progress of these barbarous villains, and save the lives of their friends and fellow citizens. [I thought] that those who retreated first, and the party who fired on us at fifty or sixty yards distant, had all only fallen back to meet others with ammunition. As I saw them reloading their guns, and more coming up than I saw at first, and several of my bravest men being wounded, the others became panicstruck and squandered over the field; the white men pursued and fired on us several times. Hark had his horse shot under him, and I caught another for him as it was running by me; five or six of my men were wounded, but none left on the field; finding myself defeated here, I instantly determined to go through a private way, and cross the Nottoway River at the Cypress Bridge, three miles below Jerusalem, and attack that place in the rear, as I expected they would look for me on the other road, and I had a great desire to get there to procure arms and ammunition. After going a short distance in this private way, accompanied by about twenty men, I overtook two or three who told me the others were dispersed in every direction. After trying in vain to collect a sufficient force to proceed to Jerusalem, I determined to return, as I was sure they would make back to their old neighborhood, where they would join me, make new recruits, and come down again. On my way back, I called at Mrs. Thomas', Mr. Spencer's and several other places; the white families having fled, we found no more victims to gratify our thirst for blood; we stopped at Major Ridley's quarter for the night and, being joined by four of his men, with the recruits made since my defeat, we mustered now about forty strong. After placing out sentinels, I laid down to sleep, but was quickly roused by a great racket; starting up, I found some mounted, and others in great confusion; one of the sentinels having given the alarm that we were about to be attacked, I ordered some to ride round and reconnoiter, and on their return the others being more alarmed, not knowing who they were, fled in different ways, so that I was reduced to about twenty again; with this I determined to attempt to recruit, and proceed on to rally in the neighborhood I had left. Dr. Blunt's was the nearest house, which we reached just before day; on riding up the yard, Hark fired a gun. We expected Dr. Blunt and his family were at Major Ridley's, as I knew there was a company of men there; the gun was fired to ascertain if any of the family were at home; we were immediately fired upon and retreated, leaving several of my men. I do not know what became of them, as I never saw them afterwards. Pursuing our course back and coming in sight of Captain Harris', where we had been the day before, we discovered a party of white men at the house, on which all deserted me but two (Jacob and Nat); we concealed ourselves in the woods until near night, when I sent them in search of Henry, Sam, Nelson, and Hark, and directed them to rally all they could at the place we had had our dinner the Sunday before, where they would find me, and I accordingly returned there as soon as it was dark and remained until Wednesday evening, when, discovering white men riding around the place as though they were looking for someone, and none of my men joining me, I concluded Jacob and Nat had been taken, and compelled to betray me. On this I gave up all hope for the present, and on Thursday night, after having supplied myself with provisions from Mr. Travis', I scratched a hole under a pile of fence rails in a field, where I concealed myself for six weeks, never leaving my hiding place but for a few minutes in the dead of night to get water, which was very near; thinking by this time I could venture out, I began to go about in the night and eavesdrop the houses in the neighborhood; pursuing this course for about a fortnight and gathering little or no intelligence, afraid of speaking to any human being, and returning every morning to my cave before dawn of day - I know not how long I might have led this life, if accident had not betrayed me - a dog in the neighborhood passing by my hiding place one night while I was out was attracted by some meat I had in my cave and crawled in and stole it, and was coming out just as I returned. A few nights after, two negroes having started to go hunting with the same dog, and passed that way, the dog came again to the place, and having just gone out to walk about, discovered me and barked, on which, thinking myself discovered, I spoke to them to beg concealment. On making myself known, they fled from me. Knowing then they would betray me, I immediately left my hiding place, and was pursued almost incessantly until I was taken a fortnight afterwards by Mr. Benjamin Phipps, in a little hole I had dug out with my sword, for the purpose of concealment, under the top of a fallen tree. On Mr. Phipps' discovering the place of my concealment, he cocked his gun and aimed at me. I requested him not to shoot and I would give up, upon which he demanded my sword. I delivered it to him, and he brought me to prison. During the time I was pursued, I had many hairbreadth escapes, which your time will not permit you to relate. I am here loaded with chains, and willing to suffer the fate that awaits me.

Afterward

Nat Turner was hanged in Jerusalem, Virginia on November 11, 1831.

Selected Reading

Aptheker, Herbert, *Nat Turner's Slave Rebellion*, 1966.

Baker, James T., *Nat Turner: Cry Freedom in America*, 1998.

Barrett, Tracy, *Nat Turner and the Slave Revolt*, 1993.

Bisson, Terry, *Nat Turner*, 1989.

Bouvé, Pauline C., *Their Shadows Before: A Story of the Southampton Insurrection*, 1972.

Celestine, Alfred, *Confessions of Nat Turner*, 1978.

Clarke, John H., Editor, *The Second Crucifixion of Nat Turner*, 1997.

Duff, John B., and Peter M. Mitchell, Editors, *The Nat Turner Rebellion: The Historical Event and the Modern Controversy*, 1971.

Foner, Eric, *Nat Turner*, 1971.

Gray, Thomas, *The Confession, Trial and Execution Of Nat Turner*, 1831.

Johnson, F. Roy, *The Nat Turner Slave Insurrection*, 1966.
———, *The Nat Turner Story*, 1970.

Oates, Stephen B., *The Fires of Jubilee: Nat Turner's Fierce Rebellion*, 1990.

Fiction:
Styron, William, *The Confessions of Nat Turner*, 1968.

Booker T. Washington
Cast Down Your Bucket Where You Are
September 18, 1895

We must bring the two races together, not estrange them. The man is unwise who does not cultivate in every manly way the friendship and good will of his next-door neighbor, whether he be black or white.
-Booker T. Washington

Booker Taliaferro Washington, known to his contemporaries as *The Great Accommodator,* was born on a slave plantation on April 5, 1856 in Franklin County, Virginia, the child of a slave mother and a white father. He was educated at Virginia's Hampton Institute, an agricultural/industrial trade school for Negro education. The Hampton Institute was dedicated to *the spiritual virtues of hard work, honesty, perseverance, and thrift.* Washington excelled at school and upon graduation became a teacher. In 1881 he was appointed principal of Alabama's agricultural/industrial trade school, the Tuskegee Institute. The Institute was a huge success. By 1900 Washington was the most famous Negro educator in America.

Upon the death in 1895 of Frederick Douglass, Booker T. Washington, already famous as a Negro educator, became the leading Negro civil rights spokesman. Unlike the militant, aggressive Douglass, Washington took a diplomatic, accommodating approach to civil rights - *I would set no limits to the attainments of the Negro in arts, literature, or statesmanship, but believe the surest way to reach those ends is by laying the foundation in the little things of life that lie immediately at one's door.*

In 1895, Atlanta, Georgia hosted the Cotton States Exposition, a trade show representing the *New South.* On September 18, 1895, at the opening ceremonies of the Exposition, Booker T. Washington delivered this landmark speech, *Cast Down Your Bucket Where You Are.*

211

Mr. President and Gentlemen of the Board of Directors and citizens, one third of the population of the South is of the Negro race. No enterprise seeking the material, civil, or moral welfare of this section can disregard this element of our population and reach the highest success. I but convey to you, Mr. President and Directors, the sentiment of the masses of my race when I say that in no way have the value and manhood of the American Negro been more fittingly and generously recognized than by the managers of this magnificent Exposition at every stage of its progress. It is a recognition that will do more to cement the friendship of the two races than any occurrence since the dawn of our freedom.

Not only this, but the opportunity here afforded will awaken among us a new era of industrial progress. Ignorant and inexperienced, it is not strange that in the first years of our new life we began at the top instead of at the bottom, that a seat in Congress or the State Legislature was more sought than real estate or industrial skill, that the political convention or stump speaking had more attraction than starting a dairy farm or truck garden.

A ship lost at sea for many days suddenly sighted a friendly vessel. From the mast of the unfortunate vessel was seen a signal, *Water, water - we die of thirst!* The answer from the friendly vessel at once came back, *Cast down your bucket where you are.* A second time the signal, *Water, water - send us water!* ran up from the distressed vessel, and was answered, *Cast down your bucket where you are.* And a third and fourth signal for water was answered, *Cast down your bucket where you are.* The captain of the distressed vessel, at last heeding the injunction, cast down his bucket, and it came up full of fresh, sparkling water from the mouth of the Amazon River. To those of my race who depend upon bettering their condition in a foreign land, or who underestimate the importance of cultivating friendly relations with the Southern white man who is their next-door neighbor, I would say, *Cast down your bucket where you are* - cast it down in making friends, in every manly way, of the people of all races by whom we are surrounded.

Cast it down in agriculture, mechanics, in commerce, in domestic service, and in the professions. And in this connection it is well to bear in mind that whatever other sins the South may be called to bear, when it comes to business, pure and simple, it is in the South that the Negro is given a man's chance in the commercial world, and in nothing is this Exposition more eloquent than in emphasizing this chance. Our greatest danger is that in the great leap from slavery to freedom we may overlook the fact that the masses of us are to live by the productions of our hands, and fail to keep in mind that we shall prosper in proportion as we learn to dignify and glorify common labor, and put brains and skill into the common occupations of life - shall prosper in proportion as we learn to draw the line between the superficial and the substantial, the ornamental gewgaws of life and the useful. No race can prosper till it learns that there is as much dignity in tilling a field as in writing a poem. It is at the bottom of life we must begin, and not at the top. Nor should we permit our grievances to over-shadow our opportunities.

To those of the white race who look to the incoming of those of foreign birth and strange tongue and habits for the prosperity of the South, were I permitted, I would repeat what I say to my own race, *Cast down your bucket where you are.* Cast it down among the eight million Negroes whose habits you know, whose fidelity and love you have tested in days when to have proved treacherous meant the ruin of your firesides. Cast down your bucket among these people who have without strikes and labor wars tilled your fields, cleared your forests, built your railroads and cities, brought forth treasures from the bowels of the earth, and helped make possible this magnificent representation of the progress of the South. Casting down your bucket among my people, helping and encouraging them as you are doing on these grounds, and, with education of head, hand, and heart, you will find that they will buy your surplus land, make blossom the waste places in your fields, and run your factories. While doing this, you can be sure in the future, as in the past, that you and your families will be surrounded by the most patient, faithful, law-abiding, and unresentful people that the world has seen. As we have proved our loyalty to you in the past, in nursing your children, watching by the sickbed of your mothers and fathers, and often following them with tear-dimmed eyes to their graves, so in the future, in our humble way, we shall stand by you with a devotion that no foreigner can approach, ready to lay down our lives, if need be, in defense of yours, interlacing our industrial, commercial, civil, and religious life with yours in a way that shall make the interests of both races one. In all things that are purely social, we can be as separate as the fingers, yet one as the hand in all things essential to mutual progress.

There is no defense or security for any of us except in the highest intelligence and development of all. If anywhere there are efforts tending to curtail the fullest growth of the Negro, let these efforts be turned into stimulating, encouraging, and making him the most useful and intelligent citizen. Effort or means so invested will pay a thousand percent interest. These efforts will be twice blessed - *Blessing him that gives and him that takes.*

There is no escape through law of man or God from the inevitable,

The laws of changeless justice bind
Oppressor with oppressed;
And close as sin and suffering joined
We march to fate abreast.

Nearly sixteen millions of hands will aid you in pulling the load upward, or they will pull, against you, the load downward. We shall constitute one third and more of the ignorance and crime of the South, or one third its intelligence and progress; we shall contribute one third to the business and industrial prosperity of the South, or we shall prove a veritable body of death, stagnating, depressing, retarding every effort to advance the body politic.

Gentlemen of the Exposition, as we present to you our humble effort at an exhibition of our progress, you must not expect overmuch. Starting thirty years ago with ownership here and there in a few quilts and pumpkins and chickens (gathered from miscellaneous sources), remember, the path that has led from these to the inventions and production of agricultural implements, buggies, steam engines, newspapers, books, statuary, carving, paintings, the management of drugstores and banks, has not been trodden without contact with thorns and thistles. While we take pride in what we exhibit as a result of our independent efforts, we do not for a moment forget that our part in this exhibition would fall far short of your expectations but for the constant help that has come to our educational life, not only from the Southern states, but especially from Northern philanthropists, who have made their gifts a constant stream of blessing and encouragement.

The wisest among my race understand that the agitation of questions of social equality is the extremest folly, and that progress in the enjoyment of all the privileges that will come to us must be the result of severe and constant struggle rather than of artificial forcing. No race that has anything to contribute to the markets of the world is long, in any degree, ostracized. It is important and right that all privileges of the law be ours, but it is vastly more important that we be prepared for the exercise of those privileges. The opportunity to earn a dollar in a factory just now is worth infinitely more than the opportunity to spend a dollar in an opera house.

In conclusion, may I repeat that nothing in thirty years has given us more hope and encouragement, and drawn us so near to you of the white race, as this opportunity offered by the Exposition; and here bending, as it were, over the altar that represents the results of the struggles of your race and mine, both starting practically empty-handed three decades ago, I pledge that, in your effort to work out the great and intricate problem which God has laid at the doors of the South, you shall have at all times the patient, sympathetic help of my race; only let this be constantly in mind, that while, from representations in these buildings of the product of field, of forest, of mine, of factory, letters, and art, much good will come, yet far above and beyond material benefits will be that higher good that, let us pray God, will come in a blotting out of sectional differences and racial animosities and suspicions, in a determination to administer absolute justice, in a willing obedience among all classes to the mandates of law. This, coupled with our material prosperity, will bring into our beloved South a new heaven and a new earth.

Afterward

Booker T. Washington died on November 14, 1915. Theodore Roosevelt said of him: *He kept his high ideals, always; but he never forgot for a moment that he was living in an actual world of three dimensions, in a world of unpleasant facts, where those unpleasant facts have to be faced; and he made the best possible out of a bad situation from which there was no ideal best to be obtained.*

Selected Reading

Drinker, Frederick E., *Booker T. Washington: The Master Mind of a Child of Slavery*, 1915.

Du Bois, Shirley G., *Booker T. Washington, Educator of Hand, Head, and Heart*, 1955.

Harlan, Louis R., *Booker T. Washington: The Making of a Black Leader*, 1975.

———, *Booker T. Washington: The Wizard of Tuskegee*, 1983.

Mansfield, Stephen, *Then Darkness Fled: The Liberating Wisdom of Booker T. Washington*, 1999.

Mathews, Basil J., *Booker T. Washington, Educator and Interracial Interpreter*, 1969.

Meier, August, *Negro Thought in America, 1880-1915: Racial Ideologies in the Age of Booker T. Washington*, 1983.

Neyland, James, *Booker T. Washington*, 1992.

Riley, Benjamin F., *The Life and Times of Booker T. Washington*, 1916.

Schroeder, Alan, *Booker T. Washington*, 1992.

Thornbrough, Emma Lou, *Booker T. Washington*, 1969.

Washington, Booker T., *My Larger Education: Being Chapters From My Experience*, 1969.

———, *The Story of My Life and Work*, 1969.

———, *Up From Slavery*, 1998.

Daniel Webster
The Plymouth Rock Oration
December 22, 1820

If there be an American who can read Daniel Webster's Plymouth Rock Oration without tears, I am not that American. The Oration will be read five hundred years hence with as much rapture as it was heard. It ought to be read at the end of every century, and indeed at the end of every year, forever and ever.   **- John Adams (1821)**

On December 20, 1620, the Pilgrims landed on the Massachusetts coast and founded the Plymouth Colony. Two hundred years later, to commemorate their arrival, The Pilgrim Society invited a local New England orator, Boston lawyer Daniel Webster, to speak.

Daniel Webster, called by his contemporaries for his public speaking abilities the *Godlike Daniel,* was born on January 18, 1782 in Salisbury, New Hampshire, the child of Ebenezer and Abigail (Eastman) Webster. Educated at Phillips Exeter Academy and Dartmouth College, Webster was admitted to legal practice in 1805.

While at Dartmouth, at the age of eighteen, he delivered his first public speech on July 4, 1800 - *Nothing less than the birth of a nation, nothing less than the emancipation of three millions of people from the degrading chains of foreign domination, is the event we commemorate.* Twelve years later, Webster was invited to speak at Portsmouth, New Hampshire's Independence Day celebration - *When the sons of New England shall, for the last time, behold the light of the sun, it shall not be with the eyes of slaves.* Daniel Webster, New England's leading orator, gained national attention with his arguments before the U.S. Supreme Court in the *Dartmouth College* and *McCulloch v. Maryland* cases.

On December 22, 1820, at Plymouth Rock, Daniel Webster delivered this landmark speech, *The Plymouth Rock Oration.*

There may be (and there often is), indeed, a regard for ancestry which nourishes only a weak pride, as there is also a care for posterity, which only disguises a habitual avarice or hides the workings of a low and groveling vanity. But there is also a moral and philosophical respect for our ancestors which elevates the character and improves the heart. Next to the sense of religious duty and moral feeling, I hardly know what should bear with stronger obligation on a liberal and enlightened mind than a consciousness of alliance with excellence which is departed - and a consciousness, too, that in its acts and conduct, and even in its sentiments and thoughts, it may be actively operating on the happiness of those who come after it. Poetry is found to have few stronger conceptions, by which it would affect or overwhelm the mind, than those in which it presents the moving and speaking image of the departed dead to the senses of the living. This belongs to poetry only because it is congenial to our nature. Poetry is, in this respect, but the handmaid of true philosophy and morality; it deals with us as human beings, naturally reverencing those whose visible connection with this state of existence is severed, and who may yet exercise we know not what sympathy with ourselves; and when it carries us forward also, and shows us the long-continued result of all the good we do, in the prosperity of those who follow us, till it bears us from ourselves, and absorbs us in an intense interest for what shall happen to the generations after us - it speaks only in the language of our nature, and affects us with sentiments which belong to us as human beings.

Standing in this relation to our ancestors and our posterity, we are assembled on this memorable spot, to perform the duties which that relation and the present occasion impose upon us. We have come to this Rock, to record here our homage for our Pilgrim Fathers, our sympathy in their sufferings, our gratitude for their labors, our admiration of their virtues, our veneration for their piety, and our attachment to those principles of civil and religious liberty, which they encountered the dangers of the ocean, the storms of heaven, the violence of savages, disease, exile, and famine to enjoy and establish. And we would leave here also, for the generations which are rising up rapidly to fill our places, some proof that we have endeavored to transmit the greater inheritance unimpaired - that in our estimate of public principles and private virtue, in our veneration of religion and piety, in our devotion to religious and civil liberty, in our regard to whatever advances human knowledge or improves happiness, we are not altogether unworthy of our origin. . . .

The hours of this day are rapidly flying, and this occasion will soon be passed. Neither we nor our children can expect to behold its return. They are in the distant regions of futurity; they exist only in the all-creating power of God, who shall stand here a hundred years hence, to trace, through us, their descent from the Pilgrims, and to survey, as we have now surveyed, the progress of their country during the lapse of a century. We would anticipate their concurrence with us in our sentiments of deep regard for our common ancestors. We would anticipate and partake the pleasure with which they will then recount the steps of New England's advancement. On the morning of that day, although it will not disturb us in our repose, the voice of acclamation and gratitude, commencing on the Rock of Plymouth, shall be transmitted through millions of the sons of the Pilgrims, till it lose itself in the murmurs of the Pacific seas.

We would leave for the consideration of those who shall then occupy our places some proof that we hold the blessings transmitted from our fathers in just estimation - some proof of our attachment to the cause of good government and of civil and religious liberty - some proof of a sincere and ardent desire to promote everything which may enlarge the understandings and improve the hearts of men. And when, from the long distance of a hundred years, they shall look back upon us, they shall know at least that we possessed affections which, running backward and warming with gratitude for what our ancestors have done for our happiness, run forward also to our posterity, and meet them with cordial salutation, ere yet they have arrived on the shore of being.

Advance, then, ye future generations! We would hail you, as you rise in your long succession, to fill the places which we now fill, and to taste the blessings of existence where we are now passing, and soon shall have passed, our own human duration. We bid you welcome to this pleasant land of the fathers. We bid you welcome to the healthful skies and the verdant fields of New England. We greet your accession to the great inheritance which we have enjoyed. We welcome you to the blessings of good government and religious liberty. We welcome you to the treasures of science and the delights of learning. We welcome you to the transcendent sweets of domestic life, to the happiness of kindred, and parents, and children. We welcome you to the immeasurable blessings of rational existence, the immortal hope of Christianity, and the light of everlasting truth!

Afterward

Daniel Webster served Massachusetts in the U.S. House of Representatives (1823-27), the U.S. Senate (1827-41, 1845-50), and as Presidents Harrison, Tyler, and Fillmore's Secretary of State (1840-43, 1850-52). Daniel Webster's great speeches include June 17, 1825's *Bunker Hill Oration - If the true spark of religious and civil liberty be kindled, it will burn. Human agency cannot extinguish it.* - August 2, 1826's *Eulogies for John Adams and Thomas Jefferson* - *I am for the Declaration. It is my living sentiment, and by the blessing of God it shall be my dying sentiment - Independence now, and Independence forever.* - January 26, 1830's *Reply to Senator Hayne* - *Liberty and Union, now and forever, one and inseparable!* - March 7, 1850's *The Constitution and the Union* - *I speak today for the preservation of the Union.* - and July 17, 1850's *Missouri Compromise* - *I was born an American; I will live an American; I shall die an American.*

Daniel Webster died on October 29, 1852.

Selected Reading

Adams, Samuel H., *The Godlike Daniel*, 1930.

Bartlett, Irving H., *Daniel Webster*, 1978.

Everett, Edward, *The Life of Daniel Webster*, 1904.

Fuess, Claude M.. *Daniel Webster*, 1968.

Lewis, Walker, Editor, *Speak For Yourself, Daniel: A Life of Webster in His Own Words*, 1969.

Remini, Robert, *Daniel Webster: The Man and His Time*, 1997.

Shewmaker, Kenneth E., Editor, *Daniel Webster, "The Completest Man"*, 1990.

Wiltse, Charles M., Editor, *The Papers of Daniel Webster*, 1974-1989.

Frances Wright
American Patriotism
July 4, 1828

I knew her extraordinary gift of eloquence, her almost unequaled command of words, and the wonderful power of her rich and thrilling voice, but all my expectations fell far short of the splendor, the brilliance, the overwhelming eloquence of this extraordinary orator.

- Frances Trollope (1828)

Frances *Fanny* Wright was born on September 6, 1795 in Dundee, Scotland, the daughter of James and Camilla (Campbell) Wright. In 1821, after a two-year tour of America, she authored the bestselling *Views of Society and Manners in America - Truly I am grateful for this nation; the study of their history and institutions, and the consideration of peace and happiness which they enjoy, has thawed my heart and filled it with hopes which I thought it could never know again.* Her book, translated into French as *Voyage aux Etats-Unis D'Amérique,* brought her to the attention of the Marquis de Lafayette. In 1824, accompanied by Lafayette, Fanny Wright returned to America. In the South she saw, and was appalled by, slavery - *The slaves are raised in the South as cattle are raised in the West. They are advertised in the same way, sold in the same way, and treated in the same way.*

In 1825 Scottish social reformer Robert Owen founded an experimental (all-white) commune, *a community of equals,* in New Harmony, Indiana. Wright traveled to New Harmony and joined the commune. In 1825 she began her own experimental (multi-racial) commune in Nashoba, Tennessee.

On July 4, 1828, in New Harmony, Indiana, Frances Wright became the first woman invited to be the keynote speaker at an Independence Day celebration. She gave this landmark speech, *American Patriotism.*

Frances Wright

On this day, which calls to memory the conquest achieved by knowledge over ignorance, willing cooperation over blind obedience, opinion over prejudice, new ways over old ways - when, fifty-two years ago, America declared her national independence, and associated it with her republic federation - reasonable is it to rejoice on this day, and useful to reflect thereon, so that we rejoice for the real, and not any imaginary, good, and reflect on the positive advantages obtained, and on those which it is ours farther to acquire.

Dating, as we justly may, a new era in the history of man from the Fourth of July, 1776, it would be well - that is, it would be useful - if on each anniversary we examined the progress made by our species in just knowledge and just practice. Each Fourth of July would then stand as a tide-mark in the flood of time by which to ascertain the advance of the human intellect, by which to note the rise and fall of each successive error, the discovery of each important truth, the gradual melioration in our public institutions, social arrangements, and, above all, in our moral feelings and mental views. . . .

In continental Europe, of late years, the words *patriotism* and *patriot* have been used in a more enlarged sense than it is usual here to attribute to them, or than is attached to them in Great Britain. Since the political struggles of France, Italy, Spain, and Greece, the word *patriotism* has been employed, throughout continental Europe, to express a love of the public good - a preference for the interests of the many to those of the few - a desire for the emancipation of the human race from the thrall of despotism, religious and civil - in short, *patriotism* there is used rather to express the interest felt in the human race in general than that felt for any country, or inhabitants of a country, in particular. And *patriot*, in like manner, is employed to signify a lover of human liberty and human improvement rather than a mere lover of the country in which he lives, or the tribe to which he belongs. Used in this sense, patriotism is a virtue, and a patriot a virtuous man. With such an interpretation, a patriot is a useful member of society, capable of enlarging all minds and bettering all hearts with which he comes in contact - a useful member of the human family, capable of establishing fundamental principles and of merging his own interests, those of his associates, and those of his nation in the interests of the human race. Laurels and statues are vain things, and mischievous as they are childish; but could we imagine them of use, on such a patriot alone could they be with any reason bestowed. . . .

If such a patriotism as we have last considered should seem likely to obtain in any country, it should be certainly in this. In this which is truly the home of all nations and in the veins of whose citizens flows the blood of every people on the globe. Patriotism, in the exclusive meaning, is surely not made for America. Mischievous everywhere, it were here both mischievous and absurd. The very origin of the people is opposed to it. The institutions, in their principle, militate against it. The day we are celebrating protests against it.

It is for Americans, more especially, to nourish a nobler sentiment, one more consistent with their origin, and more conducive to their future improvement. It is for them more especially to know why they love their country - and to feel that they love it, not because it is their country, but because it is the palladium of human liberty - the favored scene of human improvement. It is for them, more especially, to examine their institutions, and to feel that they honor them because they are based on just principles. It is for them, more especially, to examine their institutions, because they have the means of improving them - to examine their laws, because at will they can alter them. It is for them to lay aside luxury whose wealth is in industry - idle parade whose strength is in knowledge - ambitious distinctions whose principle is equality. It is for them not to rest, satisfied with words, who can seize upon things - and to remember that equality means, not the mere equality of political rights, however valuable, but equality of instruction and equality in virtue - and that liberty means, not the mere voting at elections, but the free and fearless exercise of the mental faculties and that self-possession which springs out of well-reasoned opinions and consistent practice. It is for them to honor principles rather than men - to commemorate events rather than days - when they rejoice, to know for what they rejoice, and to rejoice only for what has brought and what brings peace and happiness to men.

The event we commemorate this day has procured much of both, and shall procure in the onward course of human improvement more than we can now conceive of. For this - for the good obtained and yet in store for our race - let us rejoice! But let us rejoice as men, not as children - as human beings rather than as Americans - as reasoning beings, not as ignorants. So shall we rejoice to good purpose and in good feeling; so shall we improve the victory once on this day achieved, until all mankind hold with us the Jubilee of Independence.

Afterward

After the 1829 failure of her experimental commune in Nashoba, Tennessee, Frances Wright became a full-time writer and lecturer. Her radical views made her America's most famous female *free thinker.*

Frances Wright died on December 13, 1852.

Selected Reading

Bartlett, Elizabeth Ann, *Liberty, Equality, Sorority: The Origins and Interpretation of American Feminist Thought,* 1994.

Eckhardt, Celia Morris, *Fanny Wright, A Biography,* 1984.

———, *Fanny Wright: Rebel in America,* 1992.

Everett, Linus S., *An Exposure of the Principles of the "Free Inquirers",* 1831.

Kissel, Susan S., *In Common Cause: The "Conservative" Frances Trollope and the "Radical" Frances Wright,* 1993.

Lane, Margaret, *Frances Wright and the "Great Experiment",* 1972.

O'Connor, Lillian, *Pioneer Women Orators,* 1854.

Perkins, A.J.G., *Frances Wright, Free Enquirer,* 1972.

Stiller, Richard, *Commune on the Frontier: The Story of Frances Wright,* 1972.

Waterman, William Randall, *Frances Wright,* 1967.

EXCELLENT BOOKS ORDER FORM
(Please xerox this form so it will be available to other readers.)

Please send
Copy(ies)

_____ of LANDMARK AMERICAN SPEECHES:
     VOL. I: THE 17TH & 18TH CENTURIES @ $17.95
_____ of LANDMARK AMERICAN SPEECHES:
     VOL. II: THE 19TH CENTURY @ $17.95
_____ of LANDMARK AMERICAN SPEECHES:
     VOL. III: THE 20TH CENTURY @ $17.95
_____ of LANDMARK DECISIONS I @ $17.95
_____ of LANDMARK DECISIONS II @ $17.95
_____ of LANDMARK DECISIONS III @ $17.95
_____ of LANDMARK DECISIONS IV @ $17.95
_____ of LANDMARK DECISIONS V @ $17.95
_____ of LANDMARK DECISIONS VI @ $17.95
_____ of SCHOOLHOUSE DECISIONS @ $17.95
_____ of LIFE, DEATH, AND THE LAW @ $17.95
_____ of OBSCENITY & PORNOGRAPHY DECISIONS @ $17.95
_____ of FREEDOM OF SPEECH DECISIONS @ $17.95
_____ of FREEDOM OF THE PRESS DECISIONS @ $17.95
_____ of FREEDOM OF RELIGION DECISIONS @ $17.95
_____ of THE MURDER REFERENCE @ $17.95
_____ of THE RAPE REFERENCE @ $17.95
_____ of ABORTION DECISIONS: THE 1970's @ $17.95
_____ of ABORTION DECISIONS: THE 1980's @ $17.95
_____ of ABORTION DECISIONS: THE 1990's @ $17.95
_____ of CIVIL RIGHTS DECISIONS: 19th CENTURY @ $17.95
_____ of CIVIL RIGHTS DECISIONS: 20th CENTURY @ $17.95
_____ of THE ADA HANDBOOK @ $17.95

Name: _____

Address: _____

City: _____ State: _____ Zip: _____

Add $1 per book for shipping and handling.
California residents add sales tax.
OUR GUARANTEE: Any Excellent Book may be returned at any
time for any reason and a full refund will be made.

Mail your check or money order to: Excellent Books,
Post Office Box 131322, Carlsbad, California 92013-1322
Phone: 760-598-5069/Fax: 240-218-7601/E-mail: xlntbks@aol.com
Internet Address: EXCELLENTBOOKS.COM